Everything
you *Need to Know* about

Girls Camp

The Essential
Planning Guide
for Leaders

Everything
you *Need to Know* about

Girls Camp

The Essential
Planning Guide
for Leaders

Stephanie Connelley Worlton

CFI
An Imprint of Cedar Fort, Inc.
Springville, Utah

ISBN 13: 978-1-4621-1169-5

Published by CFI, an imprint of Cedar Fort, Inc., 2373 W. 700 S., Springville, UT 84663
Distributed by Cedar Fort, Inc., www.cedarfort.com

LIBRARY OF CONGRESS CATALOGING-IN-PUBLICATION DATA
Worlton, Stephanie Connelley (Stephanie Ann Connelley), 1976- author.
 Everything you need to know about Girls Camp : the essential planning guide for leaders / Stephanie Connelley Worlton.
     pages cm
 ISBN 978-1-4621-1169-5 (alk. paper)
 1. Camps for girls--Handbooks, manuals, etc. 2. Church camps--Church of Jesus Christ of Latter-day Saints--Handbooks, manuals, etc. 3. Church camps--Mormon Church--Handbooks, manuals, etc. 4. Church camps--Church of Jesus Christ of Latter-day Saints--Management. 5. Church camps--Mormon Church--Management. 6. Young Women (Church of Jesus Christ of Latter-day Saints) I. Title.

 BX8643.C24W67 2013
 267'.8--dc23

                         2012044970

Cover design by Rebecca J. Greenwood
Cover design © 2013 by Lyle Mortimer
Edited and typeset by Michelle Stoll

Printed in the United States of America

10 9 8 7 6 5 4 3 2 1

Contents

Contents

Part 1:
Getting Started

Introduction

So you've been called as the Young Women's Camp Director. How exciting! No, really, how exciting! Though you may have your reservations and perhaps you're feeling a bit overwhelmed, I'm here to tell you that this is one of the most fun and rewarding callings in the Church. With a little help, some crucial organization, and the guidance of prayer, you can put together a successful Girls Camp without losing your hair or your sanity.

Impossible, you say? I think not. In Mark 9:23 we read, "all things are possible to him that believeth." (FYI—that was our camp theme a few years ago. See, we're already getting started.)

Maybe we should start with the basics. Like, first off, pick yourself up off the floor and dry your eyes. Camp is fun! Remember that. Repeat it. Dozens, hundreds, millions of times if necessary. Camp is fun! It doesn't have to be scary or overwhelming. But, where do you start? How do you do it?

I think the best place to start is by building a foundation about what Girls Camp is . . . and maybe even a little about what it isn't.

What Is Girls Camp? Why Do We Do It? And What Are We Trying to Achieve?

The first thing you need to do is become familiar with the Young Women program. This should be accomplished two ways. First, start hanging out with the girls and their leaders. Attending Sunday meetings and weekly activities will help you get to know the girls and get a feel for how the Young Women program works. Second, study and become familiar with the resources the Church has provided concerning Girls Camp and the Young Women program in general. These can be obtained from a member of your bishopric, through the Church Distribution services, or via the Internet at www.lds.org. The key resources you will want to be familiar with are:

- Young Women Camp Manual
- *Young Women Camp: A Guide for Priesthood and Young Women Leaders*
- *Church Handbook*; section 10, Young Women; section 13, Activities; and section 21.1.20, Guest Speakers or Instructors
- *For the Strength of Youth* pamphlet
- *Young Women Personal Progress* book

Study the information provided and the guidelines set by the Church. Know them, understand them, and use them to help build a safe, fun, and appropriate camp.

To recap what you'll find in the *Young Women Camp Manual,* the goals of Girls Camp's are to help the young women draw closer to God, appreciate and feel reverence for nature, become more self-reliant, develop leadership skills, respect and protect the environment, serve others, build friendships, enjoy camping, and have fun (*Young Women Camp Manual,* 7).

In a nutshell, Girls Camp is an opportunity to take the young women out of the noise and chaos of the world. It is an avenue by which they can build friendships, put away worldly stresses, find joy in service, learn to recognize the Spirit, and draw nearer to the Savior. It's also an opportunity to help them learn new skills and discover the hidden beauties and strengths within themselves while at the same time gaining an awareness of the beautiful world Heavenly Father has created.

Whew! Sounds like a lot, huh? I suppose it can be overwhelming, but it's doable. And as you can imagine, organization is the key! The Church's published resources provide you with the answers to "why" we do camp, "who" can attend, and "what" the purposes of camp are. I'm going to help you with the "how."

Chapter 1

Organization—The First Key to Success

$\mathcal{I}$ am, by nature, a list maker. I find it is much easier to sort out the chaos in my head if I write it all down. I also like organization. A random list of bullet points is nice, but an organized list is more conducive to productivity. So here's my first list of recommendations:

- **Get a notebook and a pen,** and then keep them with you at all times. You never know when you'll have a thought that'll help you. No matter how genius of an idea, if you don't jot it down, chances are, you'll forget it.
- **Get a binder.** Divide it into sections with tabs. (Don't worry, I'll go into more detail a little later.) Depending on your individual needs, you may want more, but these are the minimum tabs you should start with:
  - Contacts
  - Agendas and Meeting Notes/Minutes
  - Food and Supplies
  - Activities and Crafts
  - Schedules
- **Create a list of all your Young Women and Young Women (YW) leaders.** Include parents' names and phone numbers. (If available, email addresses are also helpful.) Group them by camp year (such as: First Years, Second Years, Third Years, Fourth

Years, Youth Camp Leaders [YCLs], and so on) Don't forget your incoming Beehives. This information should be on the first page of your binder.

- **Create a "Girls Camp" folder in your email.** Make sure to label all camp related correspondence and information, then send it to this folder. This could be your best friend when you need to reference something. Don't erase any emails until after camp.

Chapter 2

Set a Timeline

*N*ow that you've gotten organized, it's time to get started with all the fun stuff! But before you dive in, it's probably a good idea to put together a timeline. We will break down the details of these bullet points in later chapters, so don't panic if you don't know what something is.

In a perfect world (ha, ha, whatever that is . . .) I would recommend following a timeline something like this:

- ASAP:
    - Get an assistant. Often, the Assistant Camp Leader is called by stake or ward leaders, but you might have to specifically ask for an assistant. Your bishop or stake president may also ask you to submit names to be considered for the Assistant Camp Leader calling.

    - Get familiar with your girls. This should go without saying, but you need to know your girls—and they need to know you—before camp. Integrate yourself into their Young Women experiences. An easy way to do this is by attending Young Women opening exercises on Sunday and participating in their weekly activities. You probably don't need to be 100 percent on this, but the more you get to know each other, the more comfortable they'll be about spending a week with you and the better prepared you'll be for their individual personalities. If you are serving on a stake level, rotate through all of your various wards on a regular basis.

    - Secure a camp location and date.

5

- JANUARY—At New Beginnings, if possible, make your first camp announcement!
  - Introduce yourself to the girls and their parents.
  - Include the date and location (hopefully you know them before now) so everyone can add it to their summer calendars.
- FEBRUARY—With the help of your assistant, put together a **camp committee**. Your committee should include the following members:
  - Youth Camp Leaders (YCLs)
  - Craft Specialist
  - Food Specialist
  - Certification Specialist
  - YW presidency members and advisors
- MARCH—Enlist the help of your committee to accomplish the following:
  - Establish your budget
  - Set the camp theme
  - Schedule pre-camp activities
    - YCL/Camp Committee meetings
    - Camp Kickoff
    - Fund-raisers
    - Certification
    - Secret Sister Assignments
- APRIL/MAY—Camp Kickoff
- MAY/JUNE—Implement your pre-camp activities
- JUNE–CAMP DATE—Finalize all your plans.

Tips for Stake Camps:

Because stake camps involve so many girls, early planning isn't just nice, it is necessary. Make sure to secure a location early . . . as in, at least a year early. Facilities that accommodate large numbers of people will fill up fast. Some of the more organized or popular camps may require a reservation two years in advance.

Meet and begin working with your ward camp directors early in the year. Keep them informed so that they can have their camp plans ready too.

Part 2:

Pre-Camp Planning

Chapter 3

Your Camp Committee

*I*f you try to plan and run Girls Camp on your own, you will likely have to check yourself in to a mental health institution by the time you're done. This isn't a one-woman job, nor should it be. The more hands you can get to carry the load, the easier your job will be, and the more successful your camp will be.

So who are these helpers? And what do they do?

I've provided a minimal list of those you should include in your committee. Depending on the size and dynamic of your ward or stake, you may need to add to or modify this list.

Assistant Camp Director

Your Assistant Camp Director is your right arm. Just as you were called (most likely at the recommendation of your ward or stake YW President), the Assistant is also called by the bishopric or stake presidency. And just as her title implies, her job is to assist you in all the details of camp. She should be present at all of your committee meetings and available to attend the entire length of the camp. Whether you divide your responsibilities with her or decide to do everything as a team-effort, she should be your key source of input and help.

YCLs

AKA: Youth Camp Leaders. These are the sixteen- and seventeen-year-old girls in your ward or stake who have already been to camp at least four times. In short, they are your Fifth and Sixth Year campers . . .

or, your First and Second Year YCLs. The size of your ward or stake will determine the full measure of how you use these girls—who, for the record would probably prefer that you not call them "girls" since they are far too mature for such terms and consider themselves, reasonably so, young ladies.

As a leader, I find it beneficial to give the YCLs ownership of "their" camp. I believe strongly in a youth-led camp and thus expect a lot from my YCLs. As young women prepare to embark on becoming adults, the leadership skills they learn as YCLs are invaluable. They are put in charge of their own group of girls—meaning, they are charged with being like a mother or big sister to a small group of girls. They are given the responsibility of befriending them, supporting them, keeping track of them, and loving them. At the end of each day, they conduct "family" prayer and scripture time in their tents and tuck their girls in with a cute "nighty-night" message.

With few exceptions, YCLs are included in every committee meeting. At your first meeting, they are given responsibilities for:
- Selecting and implementing the camp theme
- Planning the menu
- Creating the chore/kaper chart
- Brainstorming and selecting crafts and activities
- Helping to teach Camp Certification
- Implementing Secret Sisters and other service opportunities
- Forming Tent Groups and determining tent assignments for each of the campers.
- Conducting morning and evening devotionals at camp
- Flag ceremonies, campfire activities, testimony meeting, songs, and skits
- Coming up with ideas for Camp Awards at the end of camp

Specialists

Ideally, you should have at least three "specialists." One for crafts, one for food, and one for certification. These sisters may or may not be issued a formal call by the bishopric or stake, but that doesn't change their importance to your committee. Along with your ward and stake Young Women presidencies and Camp Assistant, you should prayerfully seek women to fill these rolls. Each sister should (1) contribute to camp with her particular skill set, (2) be familiar—or become familiar—with the

Young Women program, (3) set a good example for the girls, and (4) be available and dependable. Depending on the size of your Young Women program, these could be women already serving as advisors, presidency members, or in other capacities within the Young Women organization.

The **Craft Specialist** should work with the YCLs to come up with crafts that are fun, budget appropriate, and can be tied back to your camp theme. Her job is to teach and supervise the craft(s) at camp as well as to coordinate all the supplies needed to do each craft before camp. This includes purchasing materials, making needed preparations beforehand, collecting all the tools and supplies (such as glue sticks, glue guns, scissors, hammers, and so on) necessary for her to teach the craft(s) at camp.

The **Food Specialist** should help the YCLs put together a balanced menu, purchase food, and make any needed preparations before camp. She should be familiar with cooking outdoors. Care should be taken to be aware and mindful of campers with dietary allergies or restrictions. She is also responsible for assisting the girls as they cook at camp. The girls should each have a cooking assignment, in which the Food Specialist will need to supervise and teach them as they work.

The **Certification Specialist** is charged with helping all the girls earn their camp certification. She should be organized and able to bring fun activities and ideas into the certification process. YCLs should help with certification whenever possible.

Tips for Stake Camps:

Decide if you are going to be responsible for meals, crafts, and certification on a stake or ward level. You may find that you need a specialist for each area, or if the Stake will only be providing one meal, you may choose to have your entire committee pitch in for that one activity rather than calling a specialist.

Let your ward leaders know what will be expected from them so they can coordinate an appropriate committee for themselves.

YW Presidency and Advisors

Sometimes Young Women leaders think they are off the hook when it comes to Girls Camp. Leaders who don't take the opportunity to attend and participate with their girls are unfortunately missing part of the purpose. There is something about dragging girls away from the comforts of home, technology, boys, and all the social pressures of their lives that causes bonds to form and hearts to be touched. Camp is one of the best tools a leader has to make a connection with her Young Women. Nothing says "I love you" and "you're important to me" more than taking time away from your family and out of your busy life to spend it with them.

Young Women leaders should make every effort they can to attend camp. Try to get commitments from them as soon as possible, and then give everyone an assignment. If you are camping on a ward level and have a small group of girls, you may be able to use your YW leaders as your specialists (as mentioned in the previous section). If you are camping as a stake, it may be wise to call specialists who can focus on the specific needs of a large group without having to divide their time with another calling. You may even consider using your stake YW presidency as your specialists for stake camps. Whatever the case, be mindful of your adult-to-girl ratio. Two or more adults for every youth is a bit overwhelming to the girls, but ten youth to every adult may be overwhelming to the leaders. Use your best judgment and get as much help as you feel necessary.

Young Women leaders should be excited to come to camp and ought to plan to take advantage of the time to bond and develop relationships with their girls. It is also a valuable time for them to teach gospel principles. Don't be afraid to give your YW leaders assignments. Because of their nature (and the fact that they've been called and set apart) as ecclesiastical leaders, they are great tools for teaching lessons and leading activities that ultimately teach values. Thus, don't hesitate to charge leaders with the development, construction, and implementation of activities that support your camp theme. This also allows the girls to learn from their leaders in a hands-on, fun, non-classroom setting.

First Aid

As Camp Director, you should learn first aid and be proficient in it, but it is still wise to have someone at camp who is first-aid certified. If you have any doctors or nurses in your ward or stake, invite them to participate in Girls Camp. You may have firefighters, police officers, or EMTs that would be willing to donate their time. At minimum, you should know the location, driving time, and contact number for the hospital, clinic, or emergency facility nearest to your camp.

Consider holding a first-aid clinic prior to camp where each of your adults (and maybe girls too) can become certified.

Priesthood Brethren and Leaders

The priesthood is an imperative part to your planning as well as a requirement in your camping. Your bishopric or stake presidency should be aware of and supportive of all your activities. Refer to Chapter 4, The Role of Priesthood at Camp, for more details about who you need, why you need them, and what their roles are.

Chapter 4
The Role of Priesthood at Camp

*W*e've already addressed the role of the priesthood as far as calling and setting apart women to serve as Camp Director, Assistant Camp Director, and even committee members, but that is not the extent of their role concerning camp. In the *Young Women Camp Manual,* we read that "an adequate number of adult priesthood leaders should be at camp at all times to assist with security, participate in camp activities as needed, and give blessings when appropriate" (86). Though this seems simple enough, you may be wondering how many priesthood leaders you need, who they should be, and what they can contribute to your camp.

How Many Priesthood Leaders Do I Need? Who Should They Be?

You need a minimum of two Melchizedek Priesthood brethren at all times. Depending on the size of your camp, you may want more than this. If you are participating on a stake level, you could provide one priesthood leader on a stake basis then ask the wards to each contribute a priesthood leader as well. Ideally these brethren should be fathers of your participating young women or members of your bishopric or stake presidency. Be selective with your priesthood brethren, since they will serve as male role models to your girls. Prayerfully consider each volunteer's ability to set a good example and contribute a positive influence on your camp. Unmarried priesthood holders should never attend camp.

Why Do I Need Melchizedek Priesthood Holders?

It is common to hear members speak of the "priesthood" at camp, but there is an important distinction to be made between "priesthood brethren" and "Melchizedek Priesthood brethren." It is only through the office of the Melchizedek Priesthood in which blessings can be administered. The presence of two brethren who worthily hold the Melchizedek Priesthood allows for blessings to be given as needed.

Can Aaronic Priesthood Holders Come Too?

Don't overlook the fathers in your ward or stake who don't hold the Melchizedek Priesthood. A young woman's father should be encouraged to participate regardless of his priesthood office. As long as you have a minimum of two Melchizedek Priesthood holders, fathers of all priesthood levels should be encouraged to contribute their talents and share in their daughter's camp experience.

What Can the Priesthood Brethren Contribute to Camp?

Armed with plenty of water, snacks, and a first aid kit, I recently embarked on a hike with my ward's young women. It was a relatively short hike—one that I'd done many times before—and we were close to home. If an emergency arose, we could be to our chapel within ten minutes. Plenty of priesthood leaders knew of our plans and were available at the church house should a need arise. As a fairly capable outdoors-woman, I rationalized that my experience, strength, and adequate education in matters of first aid, along with an ample amount of adult leadership (in the form of other capable females) would be enough to sustain us without priesthood accompaniment on the hike.

About a mile up the mountain, however, we encountered something we hadn't anticipated. Something no amount of first-aid training or outdoors experience could help with. At first it was just an eerie presence; that sense of a set of eyes that we couldn't see. The Young Women's president noticed it at almost the same time that I did, though the girls seemed oblivious to anything beyond their giggly conversation and the rustle of wind through the trees. Calmly, and without cluing in the girls, we wrangled our stragglers in and then staged ourselves at the back of the pack. With a watchful eye on all of our girls, we continued up the trail, keenly aware of any movement in the trees around us.

About ten minutes later, as we rounded a bend in the path, we heeded the feeling to stop the girls. Further progression would have led them into a narrow section of wooded path where our ability to keep tabs on all of them would have been hampered. Only moments passed before a lone, gun-carrying rider emerged from the thick on his horse. Without exchanging words, both the YW President and I knew that his were the eyes we'd felt watching us for some time. I don't know what would have happened had we not listened to the Spirit, but we learned a valuable lesson about the need for a male presence. The stranger wasn't the slightest bit intimidated by our numbers, but the mention that we had a male presence nearby was enough to give him pause and send him back into the thick and away from us.

What did we learn and why did I share this story? In a nutshell, priesthood leadership is key to your safety at camp. The Church's guidelines are clear: you should never participate in an activity without accessibility to a minimum of two priesthood brethren. Though nearby, our priesthood wasn't a visible part of our activity. We'd considered the accessibility of brethren with the Melchizedek Priesthood (for blessings) but not the need for a visible male presence. Aside from the ability to perform priesthood blessings, the mere presence of priesthood brethren can offer security to your camp. Whether protecting a group of girls from an uninvited guest or offering emotional support and wildlife knowledge when a family of skunks lurks in the shadows, a male presence is always reassuring. Judge your situation—your location, accommodations, and number of girls participating in camp—to determine how many brethren you will need to help ensure the safety and security of your camp.

Be mindful that you're not just keeping your priesthood brethren on reserve for emergencies. Don't just *allow* them to participate in camp, invite them to do so. Girls love to spend time with their daddies! What better opportunity for a dad to bond with his daughter(s) and vice versa? And, how about the girls who don't have a positive father figure in their life? Don't underestimate how much impact these worthy priesthood examples can be to a girl.

The Priesthood Role in Certification

Most of your priesthood leaders and brethren will have some degree of scouting experience. Many of them will be Eagle Scouts. Some of them may be educated or employed in fields that relate to camp requirements.

Use their experience and expertise to your advantage. Ask them to teach some of your certification requirements.

Scouting experience should qualify a leader to teach the principles of building and extinguishing a fire. It should also provide experience with outdoor cooking, safe hiking practices, knot tying, water purification, orienteering and using a compass, and emergency shelters. A Varsity or Venture Scouter should be familiar with overnight backpacking trips and other high adventure activities.

Doctors, nurses, EMTs, firefighters, and police officers could teach the principles of first aid, the Heimlich maneuver, CPR, rescue breathing, and transport of an injured person.

A wildlife enthusiast could teach the girls how to identify plants, animals, and birds in nature. An astronomer or science teacher may be a valuable asset in teaching girls to find directions based on the sun and stars. A brother who serves in the military would be a great resource for teaching the girls how to do a proper flag ceremony. He could also help girls prepare a patriotic devotional.

The Role of the Bishopric or Stake President

It's customary for the bishop or a member of the bishopric to participate in your testimony meeting (usually the last night at camp), but if they are available, there is immeasurable value to having them at your camp for as much time as possible. If a member of your bishopric (or stake presidency) is present, he should preside over activities and spiritual gatherings. As your presiding spiritual leader, bishops should manage any discipline matters that might arise for the members of his ward. He should be included in any important communications involving the welfare of his young women. Though it is your responsibility to plan and conduct activities, the bishop should be aware of the daily schedule and approve of the activities planned (especially any high-adventure activities). Lean on his divinely appointed position and trust in his judgment and wisdom. At a stake camp, the bishops should still hold charge of their individual ward families. If the bishop is unavailable, or if a decision needs to be made for the entire stake body, the stake president should take charge. The stake president should preside over stake testimony meetings; bishops should preside over ward ones.

Other than matters of spiritual or disciplinary nature, your bishop or stake president should be invited to participate in your activities. Don't expect them to sit on the sidelines but, rather, encourage their participation in everything that you do. Keep them informed about the events of the day and ask them if they'd like to contribute any thoughts or closing remarks in relation to each activity. Be an example of love and respect toward your leaders.

I don't think it's possible to over-stress the importance of bishop-youth relationships. The more familiar a girl is with her bishop, the more comfortable she will become with him. What better way to humanize members of your bishopric than providing them the opportunity to talk, relax, and play together? Immersed in each other's company, your youth will have a valuable opportunity to see the non-formal, soft, loving side to their bishop. The bishop too will grow to know and love the girls on an even deeper level as he becomes more familiar with their individual personalities. Spending time working and playing together is a win-win situation for everyone involved. The same applies for your stake president and his counselors.

Priesthood Dos and Don'ts

- Do maintain a minimum of two Melchizedek Priesthood holders at all time.
- Don't discourage any father from participating, regardless of his priesthood office.
- Don't forget to include bishopric and stake presidency members as part of your priesthood help.
- Don't expect your priesthood brethren to sit on the sidelines.
- Do absorb the priesthood bretheren into your activities.
- Do lean on your bishop or stake president to preside in spiritual and disciplinary matters.
- Do show respect and honor the office of your priesthood leaders.
- Do provide a tent for priesthood brethren and pitch it a reasonable distance from the tents of the young women. Not only do they need a separate tent from everyone else, they need to be in a slightly distant location from your camp. Again, this is precautionary measure for them as well as for the girls. If you have an extra tent, you can provide one for them; if not, he may be asked to bring his own.

- Don't allow priesthood brethren in girls' tents and vice versa.
- Don't over fraternize. Maintain a relationship of respect and propriety between women leaders and priesthood leaders.
- Don't ever put yourself in a situation that could result in an improper encounter or relationship with a member of the priesthood. Avoid any situation that could raise question.
- Don't allow girls to ride in a car with a male driver unless his wife or daughter is in the vehicle too.
- Don't forget to include priesthood visitors in your food budget and activity rotations.

Chapter 5

Setting the Preliminary Details— Your First Committee Meeting(s)

I hope you're starting to get the idea that you're not alone in this! With the help of your committee, this whole camp thing is going to be a piece of cake. And now that you've gathered your committee, it's time to have your first meeting.

This will likely be your longest meeting, so don't get frazzled when it stretches for a few hours. Keep in mind that not all your meetings will be this long, but because you are laying the framework for everything else to follow, by necessity, there are a lot of details to get out of the way.

You can do this meeting one of two ways: (1) Have the adult members of your committee come for about an hour to deal with the "adult" stuff, then invite your YCLs to join you to discuss their stuff. Or (2) hold two separate meetings. Each plan has its pros and cons. Sometimes scheduling gets hard, so I like to just knock it out in one meeting. This also gives everyone involved the chance to have at least one meeting as a combined committee, since the remaining meetings will likely not need to include everyone. Whatever works best for you will work best for you.

I've broken the agenda into two sections: Your First Adult Committee Meeting and Your First YCL Meeting.

Your First (Adult) Committee Meeting

It's not necessarily wrong for your YCLs to be at this meeting, but let's face it; details get boring to adults so why drag the youth into it more than necessary? There are three specific topics you need to address: Location, Dates, and Budget.

Selecting a Location

Depending on where you live, this may not even be an issue. Some wards or stakes have property that they go to every year. Some stakes rotate years, having a stake camp one year and a ward camp the next. In this case, the task of selecting a location might be put on the ward Camp Director or the Young Women president every other year. There are also wards that function individually every year. Regardless of your situation, here are some things to keep in mind.

- If you get to choose your own camp destination, make your reservation as far in advance as possible. Stake-owned properties make themselves available to visiting wards, but they fill up fast. Likewise, group sites at public campgrounds also fill up fast. Be on the ball. Your first pick may not always work out.
- Be mindful of driving distance and travel time. It is likely you will have people coming and going all week. Most of your priesthood volunteers will only be able to commit to a night or two. Our ward likes to have the Relief Society (RS) presidency come visit us with an activity (this is a great way to bridge the gap between YW and RS). There may also be girls that have commitments that require them to come late or leave early. Remember to consider these things when choosing a location. A four-hour driving time just may not be worth it.
- What kind of amenities does the camp have? What do you need? Pay attention to things like running water, flushing toilets, availability of electricity, and handicap accessibility. These aren't always necessities, but depending on the needs of your camp, they could be important. Decide whether you plan to sleep in tents or cabins. If you have girls with special needs, this should also be considered. Look at the terrain and the space. Is there enough room and resources for your activities (boating, hiking, night games, and so on)?

24

Selecting a Date

Typically a Girls Camp will run from Monday to Friday, but there are no specific guidelines on how many days a camp needs to run. Consult with your YW presidency and your bishopric or stake presidency for specific guidelines pertaining to you. When making this decision, allow ample time for packing equipment and fresh-food purchases There are situations where a four-day camp may suit your needs better than a five-day camp. You may also need to consider extending to a Saturday.

Traditionally, only the Fourth Year girls and a handful of leaders go up the first day for the purpose of a high adventure activity or an overnight hike. Though this is a certification option, it is not a requirement. Depending on your region, the expectations of this Fourth Year activity may be highly anticipated. Many girls look forward to their fourth year and consider the special activity their rite of passage. If you schedule a Fourth Year activity for the first day, the bulk of your gear, food, and girls will come up on day two.

When you pick a date, be aware of possible schedule conflicts. Things to consider include the following:

- School schedule
  - In some regions, elementary schools run year-round. This may affect the availability of some of your Beehives.
  - Also try to get access to the high school's schedule for registration and tryouts (for sports or other extracurricular activities) as these may conflict for some of your older girls.

- Stake and Ward Calendars
  - Do your best not to conflict with anything on these calendars. Pay attention to things like Scout, Varsity, and Venture Camps and Youth and Stake Conferences. While some of these activities may not affect the YW, they more than likely will affect the adult leaders and their families.

- Family reunions and vacations.
  - Be respectful of families by scheduling a date as quickly as possible and communicating it to them. By doing so, families can be prepared with information and try to schedule their trips around Girls Camp.

○ By avoiding major holiday weeks, you can avoid a lot of scheduling conflicts.

The prospect of avoiding all scheduling conflicts is unrealistic; however, communication and planning in advance can help you avoid the majority of them.

Establishing a Budget

Again, various wards and stakes function differently on this subject. Your ward or stake might have a predetermined budget set aside for Camp. Your ward or stake may have means to pay for every girl, or you might have to ask parents to contribute or have the girls come up with the funds on their own through fund-raisers or otherwise. Regardless of your situation, setting and keeping a budget is necessary. Here is a model of how you might put together your budget:

Item	Cost per person	Total item budget	Actual amount spent
(Using 8 girls + 2 Leaders = 10)			
Food (@ $2.50 x10 meals)	$25.00	$250.00	
Crafts	$10.00	$100.00	
Awards	$5.00	$50.00	
Stake Fees or Campground fees	(divide total by # of girls)		
Gas (per vehicle) # gallons (estimate # of drivers) = gas cost	(divide total gas cost by # of girls)	$ per gallon x # of gallons	
Paper goods (TP, napkins, plates, cups, utensils, and so on)	$4.50	$45.00	
Additional fees (boat launch, boat fuel, special activity, shirts, PJs)			
TOTALS			

Remember, there should not be any cost involved for leaders (other than maybe a shirt or an expensive craft item). Their contribution comes in the form of their time and talents. But don't forget to include them in the actual counts and costs for consumables.

Once you set a budget and get it approved by your Young Women president, bishopric, and stake president, stick to it as closely as possible. Craft and Food Specialists who know their targeted budget amount will be able to adjust their needs accordingly. Sometimes you might have to balance an expensive meal with a less expensive one. Same with crafts. Be resourceful and keep track. Make the first pages of both your Food and Supplies section and the Activities and Crafts section of your binder a spreadsheet where you can keep a running total.

Don't overlook ward members and other contacts that might be able to donate items and supplies for you. Ask to review all committee member's receipts *before* they submit them for reimbursement—not because you don't trust those you've charged with making purchases, but to enable you to keep tabs on where you're at. Don't be afraid to make adjustments when needed.

In some instances, your bishop may approve a fund-raiser. If this is the case, make sure the girls are doing the majority of the work. Allow them to take ownership and responsibility for earning their funds. Let them plan and execute the activity with minimal (supervisory) help. Pick a date that's far enough in advance from camp so that you have time to execute a plan B fund-raiser if necessary. (See Chapter 7: Fund-Raisers)

Your First YCL Meeting

After you've laid out the preliminary details of your camp, it's time to involve your YCLs. Make sure to invite each one of them individually. While exciting for some of the girls, this new responsibility can be overwhelming to others. Be sensitive to their feelings and hesitations, but encourage them to participate to whatever degree they are comfortable.

Your agenda for this meeting should consist of the following items:
- Pick a theme (See Chapter 6: The Elements of a Cohesive Camp Theme)
- Theme-related T-shirts, pj's, hoodies, and so forth. Discuss and decide if you want them, what will they look like (or who will design them), and the targeted price you can fit into your budget.
- Crafts and activities

- Secret Sisters
- Nighty-nights or tuck-ins
- Devotionals: How many? Who's in charge? When?
- Skits
- Plan your Camp Kickoff Meeting (see Chapter 6)
- Schedule a date (before the end of May)
- Make assignments
  - Invitations: Creation and delivery. Every YW (including Beehives who will be coming in before your cutoff date) and her parent(s) should be invited to attend. Don't forget your non-member girls!
  - Refreshments
  - Decorations
  - Theme introduction
  - Activity to keep families involved
  - Opening and closing prayers
  - YW president's and bishop's remarks
- Schedule your next committee meeting. One meeting a month should be plenty, at least until you get down to the final preparations.

Chapter 6

The Elements of a Cohesive Camp Theme

What Goes into a Good Theme, and How Do You Come up With One?

In accordance with all the other programs and activities of the Church, one of the main objectives of Girls Camp is to help bring young women to Christ. No pressure, right? All you've got to do is bring the girls to Christ. Easy enough. What does this have to do with your theme? Pretty much everything!

Your theme should provide a framework whereby you can provide enriching, testimony-building experiences that allow each of the young women, as individuals, to absorb gospel truths and develop their personal relationship with the Savior. Remember, you will have girls with varying levels of testimony and gospel knowledge. Be sensitive to the gospel background of each of your girls when choosing a theme. You want something that will speak to each of them on her own level, which means it may need to be accessible to a vast audience. Don't assume that all your girls are familiar with commonly quoted scripture references and stories. This doesn't mean that you shouldn't use them as a theme, but rather that you should prayerfully seek scriptures that relate to your girls, then take the opportunity to teach the stories and help them see the relevance to their own lives.

So How Do I Go about Finding a Theme?

I'm going to let you in on a secret: you don't have to be super creative or a genius to come up with a fun camp theme. The Internet is loaded with talented, inspired women who are more than happy to share their ideas with you. A quick search will open up more themes and ideas than you'll know what to do with. Prayerfully research them and find something that fits your needs. And don't worry if you don't find an exact fit for what you're looking for; jot down ideas and modify them to fit your own needs.

The General Young Men and Young Women presidencies introduce a new theme for the youth every year. This is a great template and a starting point for your search. Try to incorporate a scripture, hymn, or a quote from a general authority to support your theme. The more "meat" you have to back your theme, the easier it will be to create activities that tie into it. Your goal is to come up with a theme that's both spiritual and fun.

A few tips about your theme:

A fun theme for the sole purpose of being fun will not necessarily accomplish the spirit and experience you want at camp. Remember to define your purpose, then choose a theme that supports it. Are you wanting to build unity among your girls? Is your message one of self-worth? Do you want your young women to learn skills and techniques that will help them increase their testimonies? Or maybe you are hoping to instill in them the powerful reality that they are daughters of a King. Whatever your purpose is, your theme should support it.

Ultimately, your YCLs should pick the final version of your theme; however, this does not mean it is their sole responsibility to come up with it. Do your homework before your first YCL meeting and be prepared with a couple of ideas for them to choose from. Remember to only suggest ideas that reflect the purpose you've prayerfully decided to focus on.

Consider having an evolving theme, meaning expanding on it or adding another element to it every day. This creates a sense of excitement and mystery to each day. It can also make a "heavy" theme a little bit easier to digest because it is presented in small doses.

Once you've picked a theme, coordinate it throughout everything you do. Put it at the top of every agenda. Include it on your invitations and packing lists. Make it easy and memorable. Anchor it through the use of camp décor. There is no such thing as over-using your theme.

Coordinating with color and images:

Pick a color or colors to go with your theme. Sometimes this might just be a random color, other times there might be a color that represents your theme perfectly. Each YW Value has a color associated with it (Faith: White, Divine Nature: Blue, Individual Worth: Red, Knowledge: Green, Choice and Accountability: Orange, Good Works: Yellow, Integrity: Purple, Virtue: Gold). You might want to consider using one of these. Don't over-stress it though; just make sure it's a color the girls are going to be proud of. A T-shirt they consider ugly will never leave the closet. A journal or craft that is hideous will get tucked away and forgotten. And because what you consider to be "cute" may not be the same as your young women like, your YCLs are your most valuable asset for this decision.

A little bit of consistency goes a long way. There's no need to over-complicate and have a bazillion different things going on. Simplicity is good. If your theme lends to an image (for example, "Treasure Seekers" = treasure chest, "Believe" = a shooting star, "Daughter of a King" = crown) use that same image throughout your camp. If you're confused about what your message is, the girls will be too.

Apparel and your theme:

It is tradition in some areas to have some sort of matching camp apparel for every camper. This isn't policy and you certainly are at liberty not to do it, but be familiar with what the tradition is in your ward so you can be aware of the expectations and be sensitive to them. There are many options for this, some more expensive than others. The most common apparel items are T-shirts, hoodies, or pajama pants. Other items you could do are baseball hats, bandanas, or sun-visors.

There are local and online resources for the design and purchase of bulk shirts and other apparel items. Make sure to order early. You don't want to risk not having your items before camp. A rush order will often cost you more. Also, don't forget to order a couple of extras. Your ward or stake may add a new girl or leader before camp, so be prepared.

Tips for Stake Camps:

Consider coordinating apparel items by ward. If possible, assign each Ward their own color to help establish ward unity and to help their respective leaders more easily keep track of girls.

Think outside the box. You may have too tight of a budget to squeeze a shirt or other apparel item in. Don't be afraid to use your resources. If you know of someone who can make shirts, see if they can work you a deal. Many business owners have a budget for sponsoring community and youth events; don't overlook these connections. You can also pick up packaged T-shirts (most cost-effectively from the men's department of your local discount store) and screen, stamp, free-hand paint, tie-die, or otherwise decorate them yourselves. If your budget requires, you could make this one of the crafts you do at camp.

Crafts and Activities—Keeping with a Theme

Remember—be cohesive. Choose your crafts and activities to tie in with your theme. This is easier to do than it sounds. With a little bit of creativity, you can stretch and wiggle any idea to fit any theme.

For example, one year we used the theme "Mission Possible: all things are possible to him that believeth (Mark 9:13)." In conjunction with our theme we did a high adventure camp that included a day of playing on the beach and boating. One of our crafts, though it didn't have anything to do with "Mission Possible" did have something to do with our day's events. We made fuzzy flip-flops for the girls to wear while they were on the beach or in the boats. This same craft could be extended to a theme or activity about individual worth (such as taking care of yourself or a spa day), or perhaps following the Savior (something involving footsteps), or maybe even something about service (warming hearts and "soles" through service). There are myriad possibilities, so be open and creative. Take a walk through your local craft store or browse the internet for lots of fun ideas.

The same thing applies to your activities. Try your best to make all your activities coordinate in some way with your theme. Some of them might be a stretch, but being cohesive will allow your girls the opportunity to recognize and remember the theme that you so prayerfully were inspired to share with them.

No Detail Is Too Small

Even the smallest things can support your theme. Something as simple as a tablecloth, a centerpiece, or even a colored ribbon tied to the tents can contribute to making your theme memorable. Decorations can be as grand or as simple as your time, budget, and circumstances allow. Keep it fun! Rely heavily on your camp committee for decorations. You could even assign this to a YCL or YW leader as her camp responsibility.

Other details you want to try to coordinate with your theme are: Secret Sisters, Nighty-nights (aka: Tuck-ins), Devotionals, and even Skits.

Tip for Stake Camps

Because you are dealing with a larger number of girls, consider rotating through crafts and activities in a round-robin sort of fashion. You could divide into groups by ward, by age, by YCL, or any other grouping method that works for your stake. Make the rotation assignments clear and easy for the girls to follow.

Chapter 7

Your Camp Kickoff Meeting

*a*fter you've picked a theme and compiled your basic details, you should start planning your Camp Kickoff Meeting. This is a meeting for all of your young women, their parents, and the Young Women leaders.

When picking the date for your kickoff, try to make it a day and time when the most people will be available. Typically, your meeting would be the same place and time as your normal weekday YW activities. Make sure you hand out invitations so that the parents are aware, especially if it's not going to be during your normal activity time.

Invitations

- **Who will make the invitations?** At your first YCL meeting or shortly thereafter, assign one or two YCLs to be in charge of invitations. Encourage them to make the invitations cute and fun. This is the first impression your girls will have about their camp, so make it a good one! This is a good time to do a "teaser" about your theme too. You don't have to give it away, but a little "hint" will certainly draw attention and intrigue girls (and their parents) to want to come to your meeting to get more information.
- **Who will deliver the invites and when?** Distribution of your invites can be done multiple ways. If you live in an area where your ward boundaries extend miles, the majority of your invitations could be handed out at church on Sunday or at a YW activity during the week. If your ward boundaries are tighter,

you could personally drop by each girl's home. This gives you the opportunity to meet each girl individually (if you're not already familiar), extend a personal invitation, and answer any questions she might have. You should always plan to visit the home of all inactive, less active, and non-member girls. Not only will she appreciate you taking the time to extend a personal invitation, this will give you the opportunity to meet her parents in a non-threatening environment and help settle any of their qualms about camp privately.

- **What information should the invite include?** Anything you'd include on a typical invitation should be included: Who, what, where, when, and maybe even a why.

  - Who? All girls aged 12–18 (including those who will be turning 12 prior to your ward/stake cutoff date—check with your YW president, bishop, or stake president for specifics) and her parent(s).

  - What? A super-fun Girls Camp Kickoff Meeting.

  - Where? Your ward house, an outdoor pavilion (weather permitting), or anywhere else that is appropriate.

  - When? Time (include a start and finish time), date, and day of week (especially if it is different than your normal YW meeting time).

  - Why? Not only is this meeting to meant introduce your camp theme and distribute important information to the families, but this is also an important time to get parent involvement. Take advantage of having all your parents gathered to have them fill out permission slips, establish your priesthood volunteer availability, get shirt sizes (if applicable), learn of dietary restrictions and allergies, and get payments for camp. Make sure to include a total price and a heads-up on your invite if you are planning to collect camp money at your kickoff. Nobody wants to be blindsided; give them time to prepare.

  - Contact information: Include your contact information so parents can contact you with any questions or to let you know if they are unable to attend.

The Kickoff Program

Opening: As with any program, you should start with opening exercises. This includes, at minimum, a song, a prayer, and recitation of the YW Theme.

Welcome: Consider having your YW president or one of her councilors welcome the girls and their parents. Acknowledge their time and commitment to their daughter(s) and thank them for coming. She may want to briefly talk about the importance and purpose of Girls Camp.

Introduction of the Camp Theme: As the Camp Director, you should shoulder this. This doesn't mean you have to do it on your own, though. Involve your YCLs if you can. Share your enthusiasm for your theme and present it in a way that will make the girls excited about it too. Remember to be visual. Girls spend all day at school getting lectured to, so try to keep them involved. If you can come up with a hands-on activity, a visual aid, or something fun and entertaining, do it! You may have girls who are hesitant about camp, and your attitude could make the difference for them.

Camp Details: (Pass a clipboard around to collect any information you need from parents.) Your specific needs may be different, but your clipboard might contain the following pages:

- Priesthood
  - You need two Melchizedek Priesthood brethren at all times. Supply a calendar for the week of camp, broken down into needed time frames. Ask fathers to write in their name and contact information in the time slot they'd like. Leave a spot for an alternate just in case someone has to cancel.

  - Priesthood volunteers can rotate in and out of camp however works best with their schedules, however, rotating around dinner time works well. This allows a priesthood holder to come up after he's done at work, spend the evening and the following day, then make it home in time to go to bed and return to work having only had to take one day off.

  - Don't forget to include bishopric(s) and stake presidency members as part of your priesthood help.

- Equipment Needs
  - Many wards have their own camping supplies (talk to your Scoutmaster for a list of available items). Depending on what kind of supplies the ward(s) own, you may need to borrow items from families in the ward or stake. It is important to make sure any equipment you take to camp, whether borrowed from a family or owned by a ward, is treated with respect and returned in good condition. After assessing your equipment needs (see Chapter 9), make a list of items your ward(s) or YW leaders don't have and ask parents for their help.

- Contact List of Girls and Parent(s)
  - Supply a list of all the girls, their parents names, parents' best contact number, and a blank spot for allergies. Ask the parents to double check the accuracy of the list and put a check by their daughter's name if everything is correct. Have them add whatever they need to and correct anything that is inaccurate. Make a copy of this list for each bishopric, YW leader, and camp assistant, one for yourself, and one to leave home with a designated contact person (someone not coming to camp). This will function as your contact list in the event of an emergency or any other need that may require contacting parents.

- Apparel Size Signup Sheet
  - If you have a sample of your T-shirt, hoodie, pajamas, or other apparel, let the girls look at it so they can get the right size for themselves. It's helpful to do this with the aid of parents because some girls may not be fully aware of what size is best for them.

Distribute Information: Have a packet prepared for each girl. Writing her name on the top can help you keep track of who you've distributed a packet to, who you've received a completed one back from, and who you need to deliver one to. There are other ways to keep track of this (such as a checklist), but this is the method I've found most efficient. If you have a method that works well for you, by all means, stick to it.

Your information packet should include:

- A cover page with your camp theme, camp location, camp staff and their contact information, and dates (including camp dates, pre-camp certification dates, post-camp award ceremony, payment deadlines, and your fund-raiser date). You may not have all of these dates, or you may have others. Just make sure to include any that you do have so that parents and girls can calendar for them.

- Packing list (see Appendix A)
- Permission slips. To be filled out and returned at the end of the evening. (These can be found in the back of the *Young Women Camp Manual*)
- Tithing slip and envelope if your families are responsible for paying camp fees. Collect these with permission slips. (Funds should never be made payable to the Camp Director or any other YW leader. Funds should be made payable to wards, and then, if necessary, the ward can distribute the appropriate funds to the stake.)

Discuss each page in your packet. You may want to assign this to your YCLs or your Assistant Camp Director. You may even assign each page to a different person. However you decide to divide this portion of your meeting, make sure to provide as much information as possible and to answer any questions that come up. Some important things you may want to discuss on your packing list might include:

- Keeping your packing simple. How much room do you have to transport and store individual gear?
- Sunscreen. No matter the elevation or temperature of your destination, sunscreen is always important.
- Scriptures. Printed, not digital. There may be no way to charge digital devices plus there is always a risk of something getting lost or broken.
- Cell phones, iPods, and other electronics. These items should be strongly discouraged and probably even restricted. The point of Girls Camp is to help the girls get away from the daily distractions of the world. Electronic media is a distraction and can quickly withdraw from the Spirit at camp. Provide parents with a way to communicate with you or another leader in the event that they need to contact their daughter.

Other items you may want to cover:

- Get the girls excited about your details! Tell the girls and their parents about your location. Where is it? How long does it take

39

to get there? Is it rocky, sandy, grassy? Should they expect rain? Cold nights? Warm days? Will they be sleeping in cabins or tents? What's the bathroom situation? Flushing toilets, drop toilets, no toilets? Is there running water? Showers?

- What kind of activities will they be participating in? Swimming, boating, hiking, rifle shooting, rappelling, zip-lines? Remember, while some girls will be excited by high adventure–type activities, some might be intimidated by them. Give them time to warm up to the idea and encourage them to step out of their comfort zone, but also ensure them that they will not be required to do anything that scares them.

- Discuss your dress code. It never fails, every year at least one girl comes with clothing that is not appropriate. Depending on your location, what is and is not appropriate may differ. If you are camping on or near a beach, flip flops might be okay; however, if you are camping in high elevations with scrub oak, rocks, and creepy-crawly things, flip flops probably would be considered a bad idea. Make sure the girls understand what is and what is not acceptable. Regardless of your location, the guidelines set in the *For the Strength of Youth Pamphlet* should be maintained at all times (including sleepwear). Girls who understand the expectations are less likely to try to push the envelope. You cannot be too clear or too specific about what will be accepted. Don't forget to discuss the consequences of improper dress (such as the inability to participate in an activity if they don't have proper shoes, or maybe an ugly shirt to wear if their own is too revealing or doesn't fit within the parameters of modest dress).

Closing:

- Address any questions from the group.
- Encourage parents to turn in the permission slips and money (if applicable) to a designated person or location before leaving.
- Have your YCLs lead the group in a couple of camp songs. Provide words if necessary for younger girls and parents who may not be familiar with them.
- Provide a small craft (if time permits) for the girls to do while parents finish up their paper work.
- Have a closing prayer.

- Serve a treat or refreshment. Try to coordinate this with either your theme or just camping in general. There are lots of variations of s'more-related recipes that are easy and fun.

Tip for Stake Camps:

Make a photocopy of each permission slip. Keep one on file at a stake level and return one to the ward for their records.

Have a representative from each ward available to collect materials from their girls. A familiar face and an organized approach will help things run faster and smoother for all involved.

Chapter 8

Fund-Raisers

*I*n accordance with the *Church Handbook*, if the ward or stake budget does not have sufficient funds to pay for camp, participants may be asked to pay for all or part of it. At the discretion of your bishopric or stake presidency, you may be authorized to do one group fund-raising activity each year. This fund-raiser should be done on a ward level and may be used to pay for the camp itself or for the purpose of obtaining supplies for the use of all ward auxiliaries.

If your bishopric authorizes a fund-raiser, make sure to stay within the parameters set in the *Church Handbook*. (Refer to section 13.6.8 of *Handbook 2* for specific fund-raising guidelines). Essentially, these state that a fund-raiser should be a voluntary effort, it should provide some kind of meaningful service, and it should be a positive experience for all who are involved.

So how do you plan and carry out a successful fund-raiser? And what are some projects that have given others success?

The key to a successful fund-raiser is to heavily involve the youth. Help them learn and understand the value of working toward a goal. You can help them, but remember—this should be their project, not the leaders'. They should plan and execute the majority of the project. Your role is to guide and encourage them.

The first step in planning your fund-raiser is to have a goal. Are you hoping to pay for the entirety of camp? Is your goal to earn enough to pay for shirts? Are you trying to contribute to your ward's camping supplies? Do you simply want to take the sting out of parents' pockets? Define your goal and pick a fund-raiser that you think can realistically hit that target.

Make sure to give your girls enough time to plan, advertise, and execute the project well in advance of your camp date. If you're trying to earn money for equipment, consider enlisting the help of your young men and even your ward Activities Committee.

Here are a few sample ideas that have been successful for various Young Women groups. Keep in mind what worked well for one ward may not be the answer for your ward. Know your area and the members and families around you, as any kind of fund-raising must only take place within your ward boundaries.

- Dinner—Pre-sell tickets to a dinner. You could either promote it as a family dinner or even a romantic date night for the couples in your ward. (If this is the case, include an hour or so of babysitting in the cost of your tickets and set aside a location that can accommodate a lot of children). Make a simple, predetermined menu. Spaghetti dinners are very popular mostly because of the ease of preparation and the minimal cost involved. You could do a taco dinner, a potato bar, or any other low-overhead food. Decorate the cultural hall to make it fun. Provide some sort of entertainment or background music. Make it a special and fun occasion, and your ward will keep coming back year after year.

- Dessert Auction—This could be coupled with a dinner (like the one described above), as a stand-alone activity, or better yet, as part of a ward-sponsored dinner with the help of your Ward Activities Committee. Have the girls (and others in your ward) make desserts and set them up for auction. Display them somewhere that everyone can have the chance to see them before they eat dinner. Start the auction when they're craving dessert. If you have a high-energy member of your ward who'd like to host a live auction this can be fun for the whole family. A silent auction would also work, but may not head as great a profit.

- Service Auction—This could also be held as a standalone activity, but honestly, you're going to get a better turnout if you bundle it with a ward activity of some sort. For great results, run it in conjunction with a ward outing or dinner with the help of the Activities Committee. Create certificates for different services the girls would like to contribute, such as a specified number of babysitting hours, yard work, snow removal, dog walking, house cleaning, piano lessons, car washes, and so on. Be creative. Your girls have talents and abilities; this is a great chance to let them use them.

- Mother's/Father's Day gifts—You can often get bulk items at a discount. Take orders for corsages (order the flowers and make the corsages yourself), cakes, cookie bags, or other gift ideas your girls come up with. Gift ideas that take the shopping stress away from men are usually successful. Preorders make it easy for you to gauge how many items you will sell and thus how much product you need to order. Make sure to set a price that makes your profit margin big enough to make it worth your while, but still keep it affordable so the families in your ward will be able to participate.

- General Conference lunches—Offer lunch delivery for General Conference. Make sack lunches that include sandwiches, chips, cookies, and a soda (or other drink), and offer them for families to order so they don't have to worry about what they're going to make for lunch during General Conference. Assemble the lunches the night before and deliver them before the morning session of conference starts.

- Cookie Dough or Cookie/Brownie Mixes—Take orders for cookie dough or make cookie and/or brownie mixes by assembling the dry ingredients in bags or jars. If you're making cookie dough, purchase the supplies in bulk then gather as a group to mix it all together. Make it the night before and refrigerate or freeze until delivery. Don't forget to include the cost of the container in your price. The same applies for dry mixes. Buy the dry ingredients in bulk then layer them into mason jars or just mix them together in cellophane or other bags. Type up the instructions, including the wet ingredients that need to be added, and attach it to the mix.

- Bake bread, cinnamon rolls, or rolls—Take orders for fresh-baked bread then gather the girls together on a Saturday for a baking day. This could be an activity that stretches over the course of weeks or months if you need it to. You could rotate the kind of bread you bake each Saturday over the course of a month (for a total of four different kinds of bread), or you could do it every other Saturday for a few months, or even just offer it the first Saturday of each month for four or five months. This not only provides a great product for members of your ward, but it also teaches the girls the lost art of bread baking.

The bottom line on fund-raisers: Whatever you choose to do, remember to heavily involve the girls. This is their camp. Give them the ownership and responsibility to earn their way to go. They will appreciate their crafts and the experience a lot more if they feel like they worked to make it happen.

Chapter 9

Menu

*A*s the wife of a Scoutmaster, I've helped plan many, many Scout camps. Through our experience over the years—and despite the personalities that make up my husband's troop—we've learned one key truth: Scouts live to eat. Girls aren't so different. Whenever we get to the food portion of our first YCL meeting, the room lights up and those girls get giddy. Like most of us, the girls appreciate good food. And believe it or not, food can make or break a camp experience.

While food is primarily the responsibility of your Food Specialist, your involvement as Camp Director is important. Delegating responsibility doesn't mean blindly showing up to camp without knowing what's going on in the kitchen. Working with your Food Specialist to ensure a great menu, satisfied bellies, and a happy budget will translate to an overwhelming feeling of peace in your camp.

You may think I'm giving too much credit to food, but my experience has been that food really does make *that* big of a difference. And it is possible to pull off a great, balanced menu—that a young woman is capable of preparing—on a tight budget. You may not be able to have everything you want, but with a little give and take, a compromise of an inexpensive meal to help balance a more expensive one, and some creativity, you can eat well!

Things to Consider in Food Planning:

Inexpensive doesn't have to mean unhealthy. Take the opportunity to teach the girls about a balanced diet. We live in a world of fast food and quick meals. Let's face it: we're busy. Unfortunately, this translates to our kids not knowing how to cook real food.

Teach your girls about balance. You can't live on bread alone, nor should you. Incorporate a fruit or vegetable into each meal. If you can afford two, do it. Local vegetables and fruits that are in season will be available at a lower price than ones that are shipped in from other climates. Seasonal produce is also healthier than its non-seasonal counterparts. Use low-fat proteins such as turkey or chicken.

Introduce the girls to ways of eating they may not be familiar with. Encourage them to try new things, but don't forget to give them familiar options as well. Hungry girls will not be happy campers.

Don't assume your girls know their way around a kitchen. I'm reminded of one of the first camps I attended as an adult. We were gathered around the picnic table starting our preparations for lunch. I don't remember what the main portion of the meal was, but I will never forget that it included watermelon. As a mom I encourage my children to help in the kitchen, so when I handed the large knife to a thirteen-year-old Beehive, I expected her to know how to use it. Boy, was I wrong!

Quizzically, her eyes bugged up at me. "I've never used a knife before," she explained, both intimidated and embarrassed. My jaw probably hit the dirt. I understood that some of these girls didn't know the basics about cooking, but to have lived thirteen years having never used a knife? Of course, I didn't want to add to this sweet girl's embarrassment, so I refrained from chortling out loud. I stepped to her side and in a private, low-toned conversation, taught her how to use the knife.

Thanks to that watermelon, my eyes were opened to just how uninformed our youth have become in the kitchen. But it doesn't have to be that way. All it takes to help our girls learn these lifelong skills is a touch of patience, a little guidance, and the opportunity to practice. What better opportunity than at camp?

Don't spend all day in the kitchen. You don't like to do it at home, and you certainly don't want to do it at camp. There's so much going on at camp, and nobody should have to miss out because they are cooking. Keep each meal time-friendly. If there are things you can prep at home, do it. Brown your sausage or taco meat then freeze it. Pre-cook your chicken until its almost done, then freeze it. Warming food at elevation over a gas stove is much quicker than having to cook it from raw. Shred your cheeses and have them ready to use. Combine the dry ingredients for cobblers, breads, or even pancakes and put them in gallon-sized bags so all you have to do is add the wet ingredients.

48

Be aware of allergies and diet requests before you go and have a backup option available just in case. There are a variety of dietary restrictions that might affect your camp. Make sure to ask every girl and leader about her eating habits. Things to be aware of would include:

- Vegetarianism or Veganism
- Celiac (gluten intolerance)
- Dairy, egg, or nut allergies
- Dye and preservative sensitivities
- Sugar-free preferences or diabetic needs

Be specific when you ask the girls about their preferences and needs. I learned this the hard way one year. Having asked the girls about allergies, I failed to specifically ask about preferences and whether or not there were things the girls didn't eat. Lo and behold, the second day of camp I learned that one of my girls was a vegetarian. Because it wasn't an allergy, it hadn't occurred to her to tell me beforehand. Luckily, we were able to alter most of our menu to accommodate her. This didn't mean making the entire camp vegetarian; it simplytv meant adjusting certain items and preparing them separate so they didn't include meat. It also meant that some of her meals became PB and J sandwiches.

Which brings me to my point: just because someone has an allergy or a food preference doesn't mean the whole camp has to eat the same way as her. Accommodate and be sensitive, but don't feel like you need to make the other girls miss out on foods they are looking forward to. Make a meat lasagna and a meatless lasagna. The only difference is the preparation is the meat. There may be meals that aren't so easy to accommodate; in this case, have a pre-camp talk with the affected girl and ask her for ideas. Usually, she will be content with a sandwich or a salad. It's okay to ask her to bring her own food items if needed.

Don't break the bank! It's easy to get excited about food and to forget about the overall cost of certain items. Meats, cheese, and dairy items can get expensive. So can fresh veggies. Balance your expensive meals with less expensive ones. Have a lasagna dinner but balance it with something like a hotdog roast. Have a big breakfast day but balance it with cereal and fruit on another day.

Shop early and pay attention to sales. Watch for case lot sales to stock up on your canned items like veggies, peanut butter, and sauces. Eggs go on sale the week of Easter; you may think this is too early to purchase them, but with a little forethought and prep work, they can be cracked open, mixed together, and frozen for months. Sounds a little strange, I know, but if you're just going to be scrambling them anyway, there is no difference in the finished product.

Think outside the box. Buying in bulk from the big warehouse stores isn't always the most cost effective method. If you take the time to price things out you just might find a better deal at a grocery store. Many stores accept coupons and some even have double-coupon days. Ask ward members to help you watch for great deals. Chances are good that you have a hardcore couponer in your ward who would be more than happy to share her information with you.

Storing Your Food

Sometimes food packing and storage may not even cross your mind until you start loading up your gear to head out. But what happens when you get to camp and have to dig through all the chaos of girls and gear to find your food? What happens when you delegate food prep and have to help anyway because you're the only one with some kind of idea of what's going on? This is where storing your food in an organized way makes so much sense.

I sent my husband on a scout camp once where he packed the food for his troop in what he considered an organized manner. He packaged all the canned goods in one box, dry goods in another, breakfast items in one, snacks in one, chips together, and so on—you get the idea. In theory, his idea was okay. This is, after all, how we tend to organize our pantries at home. But camp isn't home. And with multiple hands in the kitchen, things tend to get lost in the chaos. He came home from that camp with a whole box full of chips—not because the boys wouldn't have happily consumed them, but because they'd simply forgotten about them.

So, how do you avoid this? How do you make sure your kitchen runs smoothly, efficiently, and without too much wasted or too little food? The simple answer: organization. Let me suggest the method that has worked well for me.

The Food Organizing Solution

1. When I'm out purchasing the food, I make sure to pick up a handful of paper sacks at the checkout counter. Stores are usually

happy to contribute sacks, so don't be afraid to ask. Make sure you have about two for every meal (better to have too many rather than not enough).

2. Freeze meat and bread items you won't be using the first day at camp. Milk and cheese can also be frozen. Label each item (a Sharpie works well) with what meal it is for.

3. Separate your dry, canned, and non-refrigerated food by MEAL. Not by item, but by specific meal. Do the same for each night's desserts and snacks (if they are day- or activity-specific),

4. Label your paper sacks with a Sharpie. Include the day, the meal, the recipe item, and the number of total bags. For example: Tuesday Dinner, Lasagna, bag 1 of 1.

5. Pack the ingredients into the bags. Include a copy of the recipe (if needed) and a list of all the fresh, refrigerated (items that will be in the cooler), and additional ingredients. Instead of including the recipe in each individual bag, you could put together a small cook book by using an inexpensive photo album to insert recipes into.

6. Staple the bags closed and pack them into a box.

The benefits to this system are two-fold: First, it's always a good idea to double check your food items to make sure nothing was overlooked in the shopping process. Breaking things down meal by meal will help you do this. The second benefit happens at camp when you ask girls to gather the ingredients to start meal preparations. The clearly labeled bags remove all chance of confusion. The enclosed list of fresh, refrigerated, or additional ingredients makes it easy for anyone to retrieve the appropriate items. Nothing is overlooked and nothing "disappears" before its appropriate time.

Recipes and cooking tips can be found in Appendix C.

What about Cooking Supplies and Tools?

Do you know what supplies you need? Do you know what you have available? Make a list, meal by meal, of all the items you are going to need for food preparation. Do you need a stove? How many burners? How about roasting sticks? Pans? Dutch ovens? Charcoals? Tables? The following list (next page) is a sample breakdown for one meal. A more detailed supply list sample can be found in Chapter 9.

	Food Items	Cooking Supplies
Tuesday		
Lasagna	Lasagna noodles	Dutch ovens
	Spaghetti sauce	Dutch oven liners
	Shredded cheese (Italian)	Mixing bowl
	Parmesan cheese	Charcoal
	Cottage cheese	Charcoal starter
	4 eggs	lighter
	Ground beef (pre-cooked)	Charcoal tongs
	Garlic powder	
	Garlic bread	Griddle & stove
	Salad	Serving bowls
	Salad dressing	Salad tongs
	Croutons	Cutting board
	Tomatoes	Sharp knife
	Drinks: lemonade	Water jug
		Stirring spoon
Dessert	Sugar cookies (premade)	
	Frosting (premade)	
	Sprinkles	

I like to print three copies of this list: One for my binder, one to cut up meal by meal to include in the ingredients bags, and a third to use as a jumping-off point and checklist for shopping.

A Final Note about Food Supplies

I don't think I can emphasize enough the importance of hydration. Make sure you have ample supplies of water available for everyone. If this means toting it in by yourself, then by all means, do it. You cannot be over-prepared when it comes to water. Remember that carbonated beverages actually work as dehydration agents, so use them sparingly or not at all. And don't forget the cups—whether you choose to supply disposable paper cups or a washable cup for each girl, make sure you have some extras.

Another thing you can't be over-prepared with is snacks. Have a plastic tote labeled "snacks" and make it available at all times. I ask the girls to each contribute something to the treat box so you know there's something in there that will appeal to everyone. Because most of the contributed items will be of the sugar or high-fat varieties, I like to include a couple healthier items like granola bars, cereal bars, and even just pretzels or nuts. If your camp permits (keep in mind weather, animals, and such) you could throw some fruit in the tote too, or just let the girls know that some is available in the coolers if they want it.

Camp Food Ideas

* = See Appendix C for recipes.

Breakfast:

- Cereal
- Fresh Fruit
- Mountain Man Breakfast*
- Pancakes
- French Toast
- Bagels
- Cinnamon Pull-aparts*
- Breakfast Burritos
- Omelets in a Bag*
- Instant Oatmeal

Lunch:

- Sandwiches/Submarines
- Salads
- Fruit
- Wraps

Dinner:

- Fajitas*
- Lasagna*
- Hot Dog Roast
- Pizza Pockets*

- Apricot Chicken*
- Hawaiian Haystacks
- Spaghetti
- Taco Salads
- Foil Dinners*
- Hamburgers
- Enchilada Pie*
- Chicken-n-Biscuits*
- Navajo Tacos*

Desserts:

- Banana Boats*
- Sugar Cookies (pre-baked before camp; frosted at camp)
- S'mores
- Dump Cakes/Cobblers*
- Scones*

Chapter 10

Logistics

Tent Assignments

There is no hard-and-fast rule for making tent assignments, except to do it prayerfully. I've been to camps where girls are divided by camp years, YW classes (Beehive, Mia Maid, Laurel), or randomly. There is no one way that is better than another. As you prayerfully consider the needs of your ward or stake, keep sleeping assignments in mind.

Remember that leaders and girls are not allowed to share tents, nor should an adult leader ever hang out in a tent with a girl or even multiple girls. This is for the leader's protection as much as it is the girls.

If you have a young camper that is leery about camping, putting her in a tent with an older girl might ease her fears. One way to do this is to put each YCL in charge of her own "tent group." If you have enough YCLs, team them up. This method creates a family-type environment where the YCLs are charged with the responsibilities of her own girls. It's a great opportunity for your YCLs to learn responsibility and gain confidence. It's also a chance for your younger girls to build relationships with the older girls that they already look up to.

Grouping girls into a potpourri of ages and camp experiences can help you break down barriers and cliques that may exist in your ward(s). Be mindful of the girls' personalities and don't necessarily group them with their best friends. On the same note, make sure all the girls have at least one person they are comfortable with in their group. Every camper should feel safe and comfortable. Ideally, each girl will take advantage of the opportunity to expand her friendships, but she should never be forced into a week of isolation.

You may have a ward where each class shares a special bond and everyone is included. In this case, creating tent groups based on YW class or camp year might be your best option. Tents full of giggly Beehives can be fun for everyone. Likewise, putting all your YCLs in a tent together can give them time to plan and prepare for activities together.

Tips for Stake Camps:

Because it may not be feasible for you to get to know all the personalities that make up a whole stake full of YW, defer the responsibility of tent assignments to your ward leaders.

Ideally, despite the various activities of the day, each ward should have the opportunity to spend a portion of their day together. Don't forget that one of the purposes of camp is to allow the girls the opportunity to bond with their leaders and to strengthen the unity within their ward. The easiest—and perhaps most logical—way to accomplish this ward time is to have them rejoin each evening to camp together as a ward family. There are a number of benefits to this method including:

Assignment of gear and supply responsibilities to Ward Camp Directors thus taking that load off your shoulders.

Meals could also be assigned out on a ward level. Perhaps you want to provide only one or two meals a day as a stake, or perhaps you want to defer all meals to the ward.

Some less-active or less-outgoing girls might be more comfortable and thus more likely to attend camp if they are around the familiar faces of their ward members, especially when it comes time to go to bed. Girls Camp is a big step out of some of your girls comfort zones (especially your Beehives)—helping them feel "safe" will allow them to have a positive experience.

Gear

Just like you did for your cooking needs, make a list of everything you're going to need in your camp. Remember the basics like tents, cooking supplies, and food items. What are your activities? How about crafts? Do you have power available, or do you need a generator? What about skit props?

Break down each day at camp and figure out what your specific needs are. Keep in mind that an eight-man tent doesn't really sleep eight people, nor does a five-man sleep five. Your campers are going to have luggage that will take up space in the tent. A safe estimation of the number of actual campers a tent will comfortably hold is to take what the package says and deduct at least one sleeper, probably even two.

Make a four-columned list. In the first column, list all the individual items you need. The second column is to record the items the ward owns. In the third column place the quantity. (In the example below, the ward had three eight-man tents and three four-man tents for a total of 27 sleepers. With 33 people in camp—including leaders—there was a remaining need for tents to sleep 6 people.) The third column is to note your needs beyond what the ward has. The fourth column is to record contributions from individuals in the ward. This will help you not only round up the equipment but also make sure you return it all.

Use the following sample to create your list:

Item	Ward	Need	
Tents	3 eight-man (5/6)	6 people + priesthood	
	3 four-man (2/3)		
Tarps (for under tents)	0		
Easy-up awning	1	1	Stephanie
Camp stoves	2	0	
Propane bottles	2	0	

Items that should probably be on your gear list can be found in Appendix B.

Transportation

When we talk about transportation, there are three things to consider. First, the number of people going to and from camp for the entire week—those who will be there from start to finish. Second, the number of people coming and going throughout the week. And third, the amount of gear to haul back and forth.

The number of people going to camp for the entire week should include the number of girls and leaders. You should plan to have two adults in every car and no more girls than the vehicle has seatbelts. The vehicles need to be licensed and insured as per your local regulations, and should be in good repair to help insure safety. You may ask parents to help drive if needed.

Because of family and other obligations, you may have leaders that need to come late or leave early. Keep this in mind if you are depending on them to provide transportation. Make adjustments as needed and have a plan in place before camp.

Note: A girl should not ride in a vehicle with a man unless his wife is in the car too. The same applies for women leaders. Never should we put ourselves or those we serve in a situation that could send mixed messages or could lead to something inappropriate. Protect yourself and those you serve.

When it comes to transporting gear, ideally you will have access to a trailer of some sort. If you can get your hands on an enclosed trailer, this is a bonus as it can serve as a securable storage area for all of your food and craft goods while at camp. If you don't have a trailer, don't fret; just make sure you have trucks or SUVs that can accommodate all of your gear. Remember that your girl's idea of packing light may not be the same as yours. It may be a good idea to have a supply tent at camp to store all of your stuff in.

Coordinate Priesthood

You can rotate the priesthood in and out of your camp however works best for your situation. I have found it easiest to have them rotate around dinner time as this allows them to only have to take a single day off work. The rotation schedule you adopt isn't as important as making sure that you always have at least two priesthood holders in camp at all times. Having a backup plan or even scheduling three at a time is a good idea. Consider the possibility that something might prevent one of them from being able to make it at his scheduled time.

Create a Camp Schedule

If you don't have a plan, you might as well just be wandering through the forest without a compass. Part of that plan includes mapping out a schedule. Each day, you should have at least three meals, two devotionals, and a minimum of one activity (one will only be enough if it is a BIG activity). You should also have at least one craft per day.

Put together a schedule. Break down your day into hour increments and decidedly place "events" into appropriate time slots. Coordinate your day with your overall camp theme and make sure things mesh together smoothly. For example, don't schedule a testimony building activity directly on top of a fun activity. Give the girls adequate time to overcome their giggles and excitement before expecting them to calm down and be reverent.

Also, be mindful of meal prep time. You don't want your kitchen helpers to miss out on imperative or fun activities. The same with other chore rotations. Schedule appropriate time for the necessities to be taken care of without overlapping the activities and important events of the day.

Your daily schedule might look something like this:

8:00*ish* – Wake up
(8:30 – Breakfast Prep)
9:00 – ***Breakfast: Cinnamon rolls, ham, eggs, OJ/hot cocoa***
9:30 – Morning Devotional
9:45 – Activity
10:30 – Craft
11:30 – Solo Time/(Lunch Prep)
12:00 – ***Lunch: Sub Sandwiches, fruit salad***
(12:30 – Lunch cleanup)
1:00 – Activity
2:00 – Craft/Certification
3:30 – Activity
4:30 – Dinner prep/Games (Volleyball, horseshoes, ladder-golf, and so on)
6:00 – ***Dinner: Lasagna, garlic bread, salad***
(6:45 – Dinner cleanup)
7:00 – Craft/Solo time
8:00 – Evening Devotional
8:15 – Fire time, songs, stories, and so on
9:45 – "Family" scripture study, Nighty-nights
10:00 – lights out

Make a chore chart. Or, better yet, have one of your YCLs make a chore chart. Sometimes these chores are referred to as Camp Kapers or KPs. Regardless of what you choose to call them, every girl should have an equal opportunity to participate in camp chores. Everyone should have her turn in meal prep, meal cleanup, fire building, garbage handling, and other camp maintenance activities.

There are a few year-specific certification requirements to keep in mind when making your chore or caper chart.

- First Years must participate in the sanitation of camp, fire extinguishing, cooking two items, and food storage.
- Second Year requirements include purifying water, preparing a nutritious snack for a hike, preparing a meal that reflects good nutrition, and carrying out a flag ceremony.
- Third Years are required to start a fire without matches and (optional) prepare two meals.
- Fourth Years must prepare a meal using two different cooking methods.

Make sure your chores are balanced and fair. If you have a YCL making your chart, double-check it before camp. Post your chart somewhere that everyone will be able to see it.

Chores you may want to include are cooking assignments, meal cleanup assignments, trash duty, bathrooms (if applicable), collecting firewood, building fire, extinguishing fires, sweeping camp. Everyone should help clean up after themselves by clearing their own dishes, cleaning up after crafts, and helping with the set-up and take-down of activities.

Outline your schedule and post it. Some people like to fly by the seat of their pants, but there are others who need the security of knowing what their day holds. For the sanity of some of your girls (and leaders), it is helpful to make your camp schedule available to everyone. Whether this is via an individual handout to each girl or as a bulletin posted in a central location at camp is up to you. You could even do both if you wanted to. Post it near your chore chart and make a point to let the girls know that it's there.

Allow for downtime. Don't over schedule. Keeping down-time in your schedule will allow the girls time to relax. It's tempting to try to fill every minute of every day, but if you over-schedule, they will feel like they are running around and will likely get stressed. Give them downtime, and if they need more, adjust your schedule accordingly. Don't worry if you get off track; keeping the spirit of your camp upbeat and easy-going is more important than any activity you try to stressfully squish in.

As you adjust and roll with the flow, take the time to relax with the girls. Running around like a headless chicken serves no one. Show the girls your fun side. Show them your relaxed side too. Take the time to get to know them and to let them get to know you better too. This is what camp is for—to build those bonds of trust and unity. As a leader, you never know what the crossroads in a girl's life may be. She might need a trusted adult at camp or even sometime in the future. Girls Camp is a great opportunity for girls to discover lasting bonds of love and trust with their adult leaders. It is likely you will have an impact on a girl without even knowing it. Be constantly mindful of the example you (and your other leaders) are setting.

My most successful camps have been the ones where our girls have been able to relax and get to know each other better. There is great value in the activities that we provide, but if everyone is feeling rushed, stress rises, and the Spirit may choose to leave. Allow your camp to feel the Spirit by being organized, avoiding chaos, and by bypassing unnecessary stress.

Chapter 11

Crafts & Activities

C rafts. It seems like the words *Girls Camp* and *crafts* are synonymous, but have you ever asked yourself why this is so? Why do we do crafts? What is their purpose? I'm not sure if anyone has ever stumbled upon the history of how crafting got attached to camping, but I'd guess it's always been such. Girls like to make things. Cute things, sparkly things, functional things, non-functional things. It just seems to be something within us. We like to have busy hands, but more so, I think we like to have an excuse to sit around and chat under the guise of being productive. Whatever the case may be, crafts are as much a part of camp as the food is.

And so is your Craft Specialist. If your Assistant is your right hand, your Craft Specialist may be your left. Her organization skills and preparation are key to your success. There are Internet sites devoted to crafting, so the ideas are plentiful, but finding things that are truly useful or relevant to your girls may be a little trickier. When deciding on crafts (remember this is with your YCLs), ask the question: what's going to happen to the item after camp? Is something that's going to end up in the trash worth your time or money? It might be. It also might not be. Do you have a girl with a particular need or interest that you might be able to build on? Is there a secondary activity whereby they will have the opportunity to use their craft? Try to find some underlying reasoning for the crafts you choose. Also keep in mind the technical abilities of your girls. Push them to learn new skills but don't make things so difficult that the girls are miserable, lose interest, and ultimately give up.

Activities should be more than time fillers. It's tempting to say, "I want to do that because it's fun." And sometimes fun for the sake of fun is okay, but in the context of camp, perhaps we should be looking a little deeper. As we look to plan activities into our camps, we should be looking to do more than just fill time. You've taken the effort to take these girls away from the stress of their lives—away from the noise of cell phones, boys, media, and all the other distractions of the world—so take advantage of this "quiet" time to help them become more aware of themselves, their potential, and their divinity.

Use your activities to help your young women recognize God's creations. Use your activities to help strengthen their conviction to more fully live the gospel. Use your activities to testify of and help them realize their worth as daughters of our Heavenly Father. Use your activities to help them learn to build each other up through service and love. Use your activities to help them discover what it feels like to truly accomplish something great. Take the time to bear testimony of the things you know and believe—not necessarily in a preachy way, but in sincerity and love.

Activities should be just that: activities. Not sit-down lectures or deep—dare I say *boring*—meetings. Keep the girls active. Keep them moving. Hands-on, full involvement, enriching activities. Don't just simply go for a hike, but stop along the way and notice Heavenly Father's creations. Point out how the roots of the pine trees intertwine and hold each other up on a washed away ridge (just like we should hold each other up). Notice how those same pine trees reach straight and tall toward heaven (just like us, with their goal ever upward). There are many parallels that can be taken from beauty Heavenly Father has created for us; don't miss them in your hurry up the mountain.

I caution you, as Camp Director, to stay away from trying to plan all the activities yourself. This is a perfect area to practice your delegating skills. I like to put together a basic outline of the types of activities I think would benefit our girls then assign them to the YW leaders to plan and carry out. Generally speaking, I don't give them the details (if I was going to spend that much time grueling over each one, I might as well do them myself); instead I provide them with the parameters and the goal I am hoping to accomplish then let them build their own plan. For example:

- We need a friendship activity where we implement the theme 'Mission Possible' by having the girls gather clues (through spying or interrogation) to learn about each other. The goal is to help the girls make new friends and learn something new about some of their old friends. Time estimated: 30 minutes.

- I'm looking for an activity to do in the dark to help the girls learn the importance of holding to the iron rod or making right choices. The goal is to help the girls gain a testimony of the power of the atonement. Time estimated: 2 hours.
- I'm looking for a body image activity. The goal is to help the girls combat Satan's attempts to sabotage their self-worth and to help them further understand the importance of modesty. Time estimated: 1 hour.

After providing a basic overview of the activities you'd like to see, let your leaders choose which one(s) they'd like to take charge of. If you feel that someone is particularly qualified or inspired to teach one, don't hesitate to ask them to do it. Remember to let the Spirit guide.

You may see immediate growth in some girls and nothing in others with each activity. Don't get discouraged. Even if you only reach one girl, you've made a difference. And while it's always validating to see the light radiate from someone, don't underestimate the tiniest spark in someone else. You never know what that spark will grow in to with time.

The Secret Sister Tradition. Just as crafts are a key part of Girls Camp, so seemingly are Secret Sisters. If you are unfamiliar with this tradition, it is essentially an assigned opportunity for the girls to secretly serve someone in camp. You may choose to play out your tradition however best suits your ward or stake, but typically it follows this pattern:

1. Prior to camp each girl fills out an information form about herself. Details that might be included on this list may be their birthday and favorites such as color, food or candy, animal, lip balm flavor, nail polish color, scripture, movie, song, and so on. The goal is to provide enough information that someone who doesn't know her would be able to provide her with little gifts or services throughout the week of camp.
2. Either have the girls draw a name out of a hat or prayerfully assign each girl a secret sister. Consider keeping assignments within tent groups, camp-year groups, or ward groups to help ease distribution and prevent any unnecessary chaos. Provide each YW with the information that her sister filled out (you may

want to keep a master copy, just in case someone loses or forgets hers).

3. Set a price limit that is within reason for all the girls in your ward or stake. Keep it low so no one feels left out. Set the parameters of what would be considered an acceptable gift and what should be discouraged.

4. Have each girl prepare a specified number (usually one a day is sufficient) of gifts for her secret sister and secretly distribute them to her throughout camp. The goal is to show her love and learn about her without being caught.

5. On the final day of camp, each girl reveals who her secret sister is and some fun or interesting things she's learned about her.

You may want to consider having a central location for the delivery of Secret Sister gifts. Sometimes it works to simply sneak into tents and leave them on pillows, but in some cases this is not an option. If you are dealing with wildlife you probably don't want to be putting any kind of food or smell-good stuff inside tents, in this case, an outdoor location would be best. Consider making some kind of mailbox for each girl. You could do this as a pre-camp activity or your YCLs might like to make and provide them as gifts. They can be anything from a simple milk jug container to a hinged box or even a sewn pouch.

It's also a good idea for you to pick up a few extra gifts to take with you. Girls are sometimes forgetful, and you'd hate for someone to feel left out.

Though the program in its simple form is beautiful, I have a few variations or suggestions that might help to make your Secret Sister experience more meaningful.

- Rather than having the girls purchase gifts, provide cards or paper for them to write a simple note each day. The notes could include a thank you, a compliment, or anything else that would be uplifting. This can be a very tender and heartwarming activity if taken seriously; however, it may require some monitoring on the part of the leaders to make sure the notes are all positive.

- Take the time to make the assignments fluid with each other so that you create a reveal that smoothly builds on itself. If you assign Beth to Rebecca, then Rebecca to Amy, then Amy to Elizabeth, then Elizabeth to Jane, and so on, you've created an opportunity to make an activity out of your reveal. To be successful, you need to start with yourself or another leader. If leaders aren't involved in your Secret Sister exchange then put a YCL first and explain to her the activity. It can unfold many ways, but one that I've seen successfully pulled off several times is to give each girl a candle. Starting at the beginning of your list, the first girl would share something she's learned about her secret sister then reveal who she is by lighting her candle. You'd continue this until all your girls have their candles lit, making a powerful statement of unity and light at the end, and opening a door for you to start a testimony meeting. Instead of candles you could do something else like pass around a lantern, add a bead to a chain, adorn her with a necklace, or any other activity that would suit your purpose.

Nighty-nights or Tuck-ins should be a part of your YCLs' responsibilities, although it would be wise for you to supervise and approve their plans in order to assure some kind of consistency throughout camp. The YCLs can work together or on their own to plan their Nighty-nights, but a budget and some guidelines should be set. If you're not sure what a Nighty-night is, ask your YCLs and they should be able to tell you what is common for your region. Essentially, each night as the girls are settling into bed, their YCL presents them with a positive thought and an accompanying handout (and maybe even a little gift) to end their day on a high note. The thoughts should be uplifting and reflect gospel principles. They should help engrain the activities of the day and give the YCL a chance to bear her testimony and show her love to those she's been charged to serve.

Camp Awards: Every girl who participates in camp should receive an award. By virtue of her participation, she has accomplished at least one commendable thing. For some girls just coming was a big deal. For some it might be conquering a fear or completing a new challenge. You may have a girl who becomes your biggest camp helper or another who garnishes the honor of being able to sleep anywhere . . . including at the dinner table.

Creativity goes a long way when it comes to camp awards, and if you and your girls have a sense of humor, it's even better! Awards can be given out on the last day of camp, if you like, or you can wait until you're home where you can hold a post-camp Award Celebration. I prefer the latter method, as it allows me time to purchase little trinkets that correlate with the specific awards.

Be aware of and sensitive to girls' feelings. The purpose of awards, while they can be funny, is to build the girls and make them feel good and positive about themselves. Be careful not to create awards that might be interpreted as degrading or hurtful.

An award ceremony can be as elaborate or simple as you want to make it. Because I believe in a girl-led camp, I include the YCLs in the award brainstorming. We meet at the beginning of the week after we get home and reminisce about all of the fun things we did at camp. We specifically remember each camper's contributions and experiences so that we can come up with a unique award for each individual. After we've brainstormed ideas, I head off to the store with the intent to find something small to represent each girl's award.

Some of my favorite awards have included:

- The Snickers Award – for having the best laugh (give a Snickers candy bar)
- The Now and Later Award – for always being dependable both "now" and "later" (give Now & Later candy)
- The Super Hero Award – to acknowledge outstanding abilities or the performance of a heroic act (cape, trophy, or super-hero themed toy)
- The Peacemaker Award – for keeping the peace at camp (plastic sheriff's star badge, Dove candy bar, or can of olives)
- The Helping Hands Award – for being a great helper at camp (garden gloves)
- The Happy Camper –for being so bubbly (bubble bath or bubbles)
- The Extra Miler Award – for doing more than expected (package of Extra gum)
- The Kaleidoscope Award – for keeping camp colorful and fun (cheep toy kaleidoscope)
- The "Keeping Us in Stitches" Award – for filling our camp with laughter (needle and thread)
- The "Breath of Fresh Air" Award – for keeping the atmosphere pleasant (air fresheners)

Chapter 12

Group Gathering Time

*T*hough you will function as a group most of the time at camp anyway, there are specific times you will want to gather all of your girls and leaders together. These times will include morning and evening devotionals, firesides, and testimony meeting. Singing time and skits can be incorporated into any of these meetings.

Devotionals. A devotional consists of a prayer, a scripture, recitation of the YW Theme, and a story or gospel-centered thought. They can also include a song, daily announcements, the raising or retiring of the flag, or anything else you feel would invite the Spirit. Under leader supervision, your YCLs should plan and carry out the devotionals.

Devotionals should happen at least twice a day, preferably as the book-ends to your major events. You could do them in conjunction with breakfast and dinner, including a blessing on the food with the prayer. You could also do them as soon as the girls rise and as a close to your evening just before you extinguish the campfire.

Tips for Stake Camp:

Morning and evening devotionals should be held on a stake level. Make sure you have ample room to gather everyone comfortably.

Invite YCLs from each ward to participate. Let them take charge of the planning, but make sure they've made assignments beforehand—you don't want them scrambling to throw something together. Review their "thought" or suggest one to them that will fit within the camp theme.

Invite second-year campers to lead the flag ceremonies. Consider having a camp flag in addition to the national flag.

As Camp Director, take the chance to welcome all the girls and recognize each ward. Make them feel welcome each time they congregate.

Firesides. What better location for a fireside than outdoors in a camp setting? If possible, try to work at least one fireside into your agenda (make sure to get prior approval from your bishop or stake president for each speaker). Guest speakers could range from your bishop or stake Young Women's president to a parent of one of your girls or even an "expert" on something related to your camp theme. Your speakers don't have to be someone particularly grand or famous. A well thought out and prepared presentation can come from the most humble of sources. One of the best firesides I ever attended was held on the porch of a cabin where a young newlywed couple talked about dating. Create an environment for the Spirit to manifest itself, and it will.

Consider inviting your guest speaker(s) to join your camp early enough to participate in dinner and perhaps an activity. Welcome him or her with enthusiasm, and take the chance to introduce them to as many of your youth as possible. Express your gratitude for their time, and present them with a thank-you note or gift before they leave.

Skits. I had a young woman ask me once why we did skits. I shot off an answer without much thought; "Because they are fun." I know what you're thinking: pure genius, right? Okay, probably not, but really, why do we do skits at camp?

I'd like to believe that skits are for the benefit of the leaders who work so hard to make sure everything runs right. After months of planning, who doesn't need a good laugh? But honestly, skits are probably more for the girls than they are for us. Not only are we, as members of the LDS church, encouraged to be a "happy people," but we are also instructed to develop our talents. You may have young women who are hesitant to participate, but you will also have those who spend their week building excitement for the chance to perform. Encourage all to participate at whatever level they feel comfortable.

There is no magic formula for skits. The possibilities are as endless and varied as are your girls' imaginations. If you want your skits to tie to your theme, brainstorm "settings" and assign them to groups or have the girls randomly draw one from a hat. If you want to see their pure creativity shine, set the basic parameters and let the girls' imaginations take them where they will. You may want to set a time limit or some of your skits could drag on . . . and on . . . and on! You may also want to remind the girls about what's appropriate as young women and as representatives of the Lord.

Skits are best with props, so make sure you have plenty of them available. Assign each girl to contribute something to your prop box. Items could range from feather boas to ugly slippers to empty food containers. The more random the prop, the funnier the skits.

An Internet search for "skits" or "youth skits" will provide you with multiple sites that can give you ideas and examples.

Camp Songs. I have been blessed with many abilities; singing, however, is not one of them. Luckily, camps songs require zero vocal ability and even less talent. Anyone can sing a camp song, and everyone should. If you consider yourself too mature to sing silly songs, you are only hurting yourself.

If you are uncomfortable or unfamiliar with leading the girls in the singing of silly, giggly, fun camp songs, assign the task to someone else. I love to let my YCLs take charge of the fireside entertainment, including singing. Often they won't even need encouragement or guidance, but if they do, provide them with a list of songs and perhaps even a book of lyrics. If your budget allows, consider printing a book of camp songs for every girl. If it doesn't, print out a few copies for the girls to share—your first-years will love you for this! Hold onto the books from year to year and use them over and over again.

The *Young Women Camp Manual* contains the words and music to some appropriate popular camp songs. I've included the words to some others in Appendix D.

Testimony Meeting—the pinnacle of camp. Customarily, a testimony meeting is held around the campfire on the last night of camp. For many girls, this could be the first time they publically share their testimony. For others, it could be the first time they recognize the Spirit. Don't underestimate the power of this meeting. And don't rush it. Allow the girls to feel the Spirit even if they choose not to share their feelings. Allow them the time to process and appreciate the feelings they've been building toward all week.

Help to create an appropriate atmosphere for the Spirit to be present. If your testimony meeting is following the presentation of skits and the singing of a few fun songs, redirect the mood through a couple softer songs or hymns. Share a spiritual thought (either from yourself or another of the adult leaders) to mellow the mood, and then open the floor to all who want to share whatever they are feeling.

Consider having a short fireside in conjunction with your testimony meeting. Or perhaps invite your bishopric(s) and stake presidency to attend and offer a spiritual thought to help set the mood. Be cautious, however, not to start too late in the evening or to include too much buildup. Remember, you are at the end of your week and the girls—and yourself too—are more than likely running on fumes. Don't overshadow or crowd your testimony meeting by over-scheduling the attention spans of any of your participants. You don't want girls falling asleep in their camp chairs because the night has gone too long. Too much of a good thing is still too much.

If you are camping on a stake level, try to allot enough time for both a stake testimony meeting and a ward one. Some girls will be more than comfortable bearing their hearts to a large group, but others will be much more comfortable in the intimate setting of their ward family. Allowing the opportunity for both is important, but if you are tight on time and can only do one, do it on a ward level.

Have an idea of how you'd like to close the meeting when the time is appropriate. Don't jump up and ask for a closing prayer the first time you experience a span of silence. You may want to ask your Young Women president or bishop to conduct the meeting, thus allowing them to set the parameters.

A note about prayers and food blessings: Respect the role of your young women class presidents by allowing them the opportunity to serve and lead their girls while at camp. A simple way to do this is to allow each of your class presidents the chance to be in charge of assigning the prayer or food blessing. Rotate through all three of your classes to give adequate opportunity for each president.

If a member of your bishopric (or stake presidency) is present, invite him to preside over spiritual gatherings, food blessings, and devotionals. Invite him to contribute his thoughts at the conclusion to all activities.

Chapter 13

Certification

*T*he *Young Women Camp Manual* gives a full outline of all the certification for each camp year. Refer to it for details, be familiar with it, and organize your efforts in a manner that works best for your camp.

You may choose to do all of your certification at camp. If you do, make sure to set aside ample time for each certification as well as some downtime so the girls don't get overwhelmed or bored. Ways that this can be accomplished include dividing the certification activities by camp year, dividing the activities by functionality (such as cooking, first aid, and so on), or even having a round-robin that would include everything for everybody. Be aware that some of the requirements span over the course of days, so you will need to plan your schedule to include enough time to do them. This includes a daily scripture study of at least fifteen minutes. Implement the cooking requirements (for all camp levels) into your meal preparations whenever possible. There's no better teaching tool than hands-on experience.

I prefer to do some of my certifications before camp. Doing this serves two purposes. First, it teaches skills and instills some camping and outdoor knowledge before we show up at camp. Some of the girls will likely be unfamiliar with camping safety and first aid, so teaching them beforehand will allow them to be prepared as soon as their shoes touch the dirt. The second reason I like to do some certification before camp is that by doing so we are able to free up time at camp. As I mentioned before, there is nothing worse than an overscheduled, overstressed camp.

Regardless of when you do your certifications, try to keep them fun. Do hands-on activities that keep the girls involved. Try a treasure hunt to learn how to read a compass. Have a relay with first aid transportation techniques. Script a mock disaster to challenge the girls' first-aid knowledge. Play a game. Stage "incidents" or "road blocks" along a hike that require the passing of a requirement before progressing further along the route. Be creative and keep it fun.

To make your planning easier, I've broken down the certification requirements by activity type and camp year. You will see that many of the certifications coordinate across the different camp levels. Using girls with more camp experience to teach your younger girls certifications provides a great review for them. For example, planning a first-aid night allows you to teach the required certifications for all the camp levels in one organized meeting.

Certifications That Can Be Done before Camp

Hiking:

First Year Requirement	Help plan and participate in a three-mile hike. Learn what to do if you become lost.
Second Year Requirement	Help to plan and participate in a five-mile hike. Plan and carry a nutritious meal for the hike.
Third Year Requirement	Participate in an organized hike.
Fourth Year Requirement	Help to organize and participate in a nature walk or hike for younger campers.

Water Purification:

Second Year Requirement	Demonstrate two methods for purifying drinking water.
Third Year Requirement	Learn what to do if the water in your camp were unsafe to drink. Describe how you would make it safe. If there is a stream, lake, or ocean near your campsite, survey the area and report any sources of pollution. Where possible, correct these problems.

Orienteering Skills:

Second Year Requirement	Demonstrate how to find directions by observing the sun and stars.
Third Year Requirement	Learn how to use a compass to find directions. Participate in an orienteering activity.

treasure hunt

Nature Observation:

First Year Requirement	(*optional) Spend at least thirty minutes in nature observing Heavenly Father's creations that you can see, hear, smell, or touch. (See the "optional" section for more details.)
	(*optional) Identify six kinds of plants and three kinds of animals. (See the "optional" section for more details.)
Second Year Requirement	Learn about the various kinds of cloud formations. If possible, identify three different formations during your stay at camp.
	(*optional) Spend at least thirty minutes observing Heavenly Father's creations. (See the "optional" section for more details.)
Third Year Requirement	Spend time observing an event in nature. It could be a sunrise or a sunset, the movement of clouds, or a rainbow. With artwork, poetry, song, dance, or the written word, express your thoughts. You may want to share your thoughts with others.
Fourth Year Requirement	Spend some time observing the night sky. Identify two or more constellations. Then read Doctrine and Covenants 88: 42–44; Moses 1: 37–39; and Doctrine and Covenants 67:2. Share with a leader or a group your thoughts about what you observed and what you read in these scriptures.

Emergency Prep and First Aid:

First Year Requirement	Explain the purpose of first aid, and learn the first four steps to take when treating accident victims.
	Demonstrate how to perform the Heimlich maneuver to help a person who is choking.
	Demonstrate how to give first aid for excessive bleeding and poisoning.
	Learn how to fold a cravat bandage. Demonstrate the uses of the bandage.
	Learn what should go in a basic first-aid kit and the use of each item.

Second Year Requirement	Learn how to signal for help in the outdoors. Identify local authorities who could provide help, such as park rangers, local emergency personnel, ski patrols, and search and rescue teams. Learn how to contact the authorities.
	Demonstrate how to treat someone who has fainted or is in shock.
	Demonstrate how to give first aid for heat exhaustion and heat stroke or for hypothermia and frostbite, depending on local circumstances.
	Demonstrate how to give rescue breathing.
	(*optional) Learn to identify poisonous and edible plants in your area. (See the "optional" section for more details.)
Third Year Requirement	Show how to give emergency first aid for insect bites or tings, burns, blisters, and snakebites if snakes are common in your area.
	Demonstrate how to give cardiopulmonary resuscitation (CPR).
	(*optional) Learn the guidelines for safety during hiking or waters sports. (See the "optional" section for more details.)
	(*optional) Learn how to construct three types of emergency shelters. (See the "optional" section for more details.)
Fourth Year Requirement	Learn what to do for your safety during severe weather conditions in your area such as lightning, tornadoes, typhoons, avalanches, or floods.
	Describe the signs of a broken bone. Demonstrate first aid procedures for handling broken bones.
	Learn and demonstrate four methods for transporting someone who is inured.
	Review first-aid skills for the first three certification levels. Demonstrate the Heimlich maneuver, rescue breathing, and CPR.

Environmental Awareness:

First Year Requirement	Learn the basic principles of sanitation for your camp setting. Learn how to correctly dispose of refuse while hiking. Learn how to dispose of garbage at camp and leave the campsite cleaner than you found it. Follow these principles during your stay at camp.
	(*optional) Help implement a recycling program at camp. (See the "optional" section for more details.)
Third Year Requirement	Learn one way to help preserve and protect the environment in your area. Use what you learn to make an improvement in your area.
Fourth Year Requirement	Demonstrate or teach ways to protect the environment in your area. Carry out a project that helps to preserve or restore the area.
	(*optional) Learn something new about nature and teach it to your group. (See the "optional" section for more details.)

Skill Development:

First Year Requirement	(*optional) Learn how to tie different knots and when to use them. (See the "optional" section for more details.)
Second Year Requirement	(*optional) Knife use and safety. (See the "optional" section for more details.)
Fourth Year Requirement	(*optional) Make a bedroll or emergency ground bed. (See the "optional" section for more details.)
	(*optional) Plan and participate in an overnight backpacking trip or other adventuring activity.

Certifications That Should Be Done While at Camp

Scripture Study:

First Year Requirement	Each day while in camp, find a quiet spot and read form the scriptures for at least fifteen minutes. Read about the Creation as found in Moses 2:1–31 or Genesis 1:1–31. After the Lord created the earth, He surveyed his work and saw that is was very good. Share your thoughts about God's creations with a leader or a friend.
Second Year Requirement	Each day while in camp, find a quiet spot and read from the scriptures for at least fifteen minutes. Include in your reading Joseph Smith History 1:1–20, the account of Joseph Smith's prayer in the Sacred Grove. Record or share your thoughts about Joseph Smith and his vision.
Third Year Requirement	Each day while in camp, find a quiet spot and read from the scriptures for at least fifteen minutes. Include Mosiah 18:1–17 in your reading. Review the covenants the people in the Book of Mormon made at the time of their baptism and the feelings they had. Record your feelings about your baptism.
Fourth Year Requirement	Each day while in camp, find a quiet spot and read from the scriptures for at least fifteen minutes. Include in your reading Matthew 26:36–46, an account of the events in the Garden of Gethsemane. Record your feelings about what Christ did for you.

Fire:

First Year Requirement	Learn the fire regulations for you camping area. Learn the procedures for properly extinguishing fire.
Second Year Requirement	(*optional) Learn how to build two kinds of fires. (See the "optional" section for more details.)
Third Year Requirement	Demonstrate the procedures for extinguishing accidental fires, such as those caused by grease igniting while cooking, clothing catching on fire, or wind blowing sparks into dry vegetation.
	Learn two ways to start a fire without using matches. Learn how to waterproof matches.

Food:

First Year Requirement	Cook at least two items using fire or a camp stove.
	Learn the basic principles of storing and preparing food in the outdoors.
Second Year Requirement	Learn the basic principles of good nutrition. Plan and prepare one meal at camp.
Third Year Requirement	(*optional) Try two types of outdoor cooking. (See the "optional" section for more details.)
Fourth Year Requirement	Prepare a meal using two different methods of cooking.

Service:

First Year Requirement	Find an opportunity to serve another camper or leader. Help with something you are not assigned to do. This could include helping with camp chores such as cleaning the camp area or preparing a meal and cleaning up afterword.
Second Year Requirement	Find an opportunity to serve another camper or leader. Help with something you are not assigned to do. This could include helping with camp chores such as cleaning the camp area or preparing a meal and cleaning up afterward.
Third Year Requirement	Complete an assignment made by your stake or ward camp director.
	Find out who in the camp has a need; then help to fill that need.
	(*optional) Volunteer to help a younger camper with her certification. (See the "optional" section for more details.)
Fourth Year Requirement	Discuss a need in the camp with the camp director and, with the help of the Youth Camp Leaders, develop a plan to fill that need.
	(*optional) Develop a project to help campers with disabilities. (See the "optional" section for more details.)

Songs, Skits, and Game Leadership:

First Year Requirement	Help to plan and present a song or skit on a topic such as the camp theme; the Young Women values, motto, or logo; or stories from the scriptures.
Second Year Requirement	Help plan and participate in a flag-raising ceremony or devotional.
	Help to plan and present a song or skit on a topic such as the camp them; the Young Women values, motto, or logo; or stories from the scriptures.
Third Year Requirement	Teach a song or a game to a group.
Fourth Year Requirement	Help plan an activity for the whole camp or your own group that will help the campers get to know each other. Involve everyone.
	Help to plan and present a song or skit on a topic such as the camp theme; the Young Women values, motto, or logo; or stories from the scriptures.

In addition to the required activities, each camper must complete two of the following options under her camp year level:

First Year Requirement	Spend at least 30 minutes in nature observing Heavenly Father's creations that you can see, hear, smell, or touch. Thank Heavenly Father for the beauty around you. Share your thoughts about nature with a leader or friend.
	Sort used glass, plastic, and aluminum containers, and see that they are turned in for recycling after camp.
	Learn to identify six kinds of plants and three kinds of animals, birds, or fish that are found in our area. Observe interesting details about each one.
Second Year Requirement	Spend at least 30 minutes in nature observing Heavenly Father's creations. Thank Heavenly Father for the beauty around you. Record what you've seen and your feelings about it. Share your thoughts with others.
	Learn how to build two kinds of fires. If fire regulations permit, light them and extinguish them properly.
	Identify three to five poisonous plants and three to five edible plants in your area.
	Demonstrate how to properly sharpen, use, and care for a knife.

Third Year Requirement	Learn the guidelines for safety during hiking or water sports. Teach these guidelines to a group.
	Learn how to construct three types of emergency shelters, including those made with a tarp or other waterproof material.
	Try two types of outdoor cooking that you have not tried before, such as pit cooking, cooking without utensils, or cooking with a Dutch oven or reflector oven.
	Volunteer to help a younger camper or one with disabilities complete a requirement for certification.
Fourth Year Requirement	With another camper or by yourself, learn something new about nature and teach it to you group.
	Develop a project to help campers with disabilities. For example, develop a nature trail or an experience with nature for someone who is blind or in a wheelchair or who has other special needs.
	Demonstrate how to make a bedroll or an emergency ground bed from materials that are not living. Plan and participate in an overnight backpacking trip or other adventuring activity.

Tips for Stake Camps:

Tackling certification for hundreds of girls can prove to be quite a challenge. Consider leaving certification in the hands of your ward leaders. Coordinate with them as to what kinds of activities will be available at camp so they can plan their certifications accordingly.

Another way to tackle certification for a large group would be to have a Certification Specialist for each camp level. Charge each specialist with planning and carrying out the certification requirements for her group of girls.

If you choose to do certification as a large group at camp, try staging a mock disaster or a relay race. Making certification a fun activity will help the girls to not feel overburdened or bored by the requirements.

Each young women and leader should have her own copy of the *Young Women Camp Manual*. As she passes off each requirement you should provide her with a signature on the appropriate line. Use the following chart as a quick reference guide for your planning or as a checklist to keep track of where you are with certification. Details for each requirement can be found earlier in this chapter or in the *Young Women Camp Manual*.

First Years	Second Years	Third Years	Fourth Years
Three mile hike	Five mile hike (prep nutritious snacks)	Hike	Plan and participate in a hike for younger girls
• Learn the purpose of first aid & demonstrate • Heimlich maneuver • Cravat bandage • What goes in a first aid kit? • Treat excessive bleeding and poisoning	• Learn how to signal for help • How to treat shock • First aid for heat exhaustion and heat stroke • Rescue breathing	• First aid for insect bites, stings, burns, snake bites • Demonstrate CPR	• Safety during lightning, tornadoes, floods • First Aid for broken bone • Four methods of transporting an injured person • Review First Aid for levels 1–3 • Teach what to do if lost
	Water purification methods	How to make a water source safe	
Observe nature for 30 minutes (optional)	• Find direction from the sun and stars • Observe and identify cloud formations	Compass activity	Identify two or more constellations
		How to preserve and protect environment	Demonstrate ways to protect environment
Daily scripture study for 15 minutes.	Daily scripture study for 15 minutes.	Daily scripture study for 15 minutes.	Daily scripture study for 15 minutes.
• Sanitation of camp • Recycle at camp (optional)	Plan and participate in a flag ceremony	Write about nature observation	

Fire regulations and extinguishing	(Build two types of fires • optional, see below)	• Learn how to start a fire without matches • Extinguish accidental fires	
• Cook two items with a fire or a camp stove • Store and prepare food outdoors	Good nutrition & prep one meal	(Two types of outdoor cooking • optional, see below)	• Prep a meal using two different methods
Serve another camper or camp leader	Serve another camper or camp leader	• Complete an assignment from the camp leader • Fill a camp need	• Fill a camp need
Help plan and present a song or skit	Help plan and present a song or skit	Help plan and present a song or skit	Help plan and present a song or skit
		Teach a song or game to the group	Plan a get-to-know you activity for group
Choose two or more of the following: • Observe nature for 30 min. • Recycle camp items • Learn how to tie knots • Identify plants & animals	Choose two or more of the following: • Observe nature for 30 min. • Identify three poisonous and three edible plants • Sharpen, use, and care for a knife. • Build two types of fires	Choose two or more of the following: • Safety guidelines for hiking or water sports • Three types of emergency structures • Two types of outdoor cooking • Help younger camper with certification	Choose two or more of the following: • Learn something about nature and teach it to the group • Develop a project for a camper with disabilities • Participate in an overnight backpacking trip.

Sources:

Young Women Camp Manual (Salt Lake City: Intellectual Reserve, 2002) 8–18.

Chapter 14

And We're Off!

*W*hew! You've spent months of planning and preparation and now the time is near. Either you're nearly a basket case at this point or you're feeling strangely calm. That calm feeling is likely as unnerving as is the frantic one, but don't fret. Sanity is just a few checklists away.

In the Days before You Leave:

1. Double check all of your **permission slips** (available in the back of the *Young Women Camp Manual*). Every girl needs a signed permission slip even if her parent(s) will be at camp. Make sure the information on them is current and legible. Keep the original for yourself, but provide a copy to each ward-level camp director as well as one to each driver for the passengers in his or her vehicle.

2. Communicate with those who've offered to provide **transportation** as well as those who've volunteered as your **Melchizedek Priesthood representatives** and anyone else who will be coming and going to camp. Give them written handouts that include maps, driving directions, and pertinent dates and times. Include contact numbers where they can reach you if needed. Have a contact person at home who can help coordinate alternate drivers and priesthood if the need arises.

3. Have a **current roster** of *everyone* who will be attending camp, including those who will be coming and going as guests. Make sure you have a contact number for each girl, leader, and other

camp guest. Keep this list in the front of your binder where it will be easily found. Provide a copy to each member of your camp committee.

4. **Purchase your food** and organize it. If your food specialist is doing this, ask her if she needs help. Offer whatever assistance she needs. Be available to shop with her if needed. If you're storing food in a garage, keep in mind the outdoor temperature and the possibility of little creatures or bugs. Always store food safely.

5. **Arrange a drop-off location and time for equipment.** Having the girls drop off their equipment the day or evening before will allow time to organize it as well as aid in your ability to leave on time. If you have an enclosed trailer, let them load their own stuff. Remind them to label everything and provide some tape and a marker for them to do so. If you have them contributing a treat to your snack bucket, have the bucket available for them to put it in when they drop off their equipment.

6. **Use wisdom when packing your gear.** Think ahead to what you're going to need to use first when you get to your campsite. Are you going to be eating right away? Do you need a stove or access to your coolers? Or are you having the girls bring a sack lunch from home? Remember, the first things you pack are the last things you will unpack. If setting up tents is your first item of business when you reach camp, they should probably be the last thing you pack for transport.

Hitting the Road:

1. **Leave on time.** Set a meeting time and designate a place to gather and communicate it well. Make sure everyone knows well ahead of time, but still be prepared to make some last-minute phone calls to gather forgetful girls. Establish a departure time and stick to it as closely as you can. A late arrival could affect the rest of your events for the day. Allow time to do roll-call and have a prayer. You may want to consider sharing a thought or reciting the Young Women theme as well.

2. **Be Prepared.** Be ready when the girls start arriving. If needed, have your leaders come early to help with any last-minute details. Start your camp off on the right foot by being ready and organized so your focus can be on the girls.

Arrival:

1. **Welcome** your campers with a quick activity to set the tone and expectations for camp. Say a prayer as soon as everyone has arrived and open with a small activity, such as a get-to-know you game or a friendshipping activity.

2. **Give an overview of your facilities.** Help your campers become familiar with your camp area. Point out important things such as restrooms, gathering areas, and hazards. Establish rules and guidelines for areas that are off-limits.

3. **Assist in camp set-up,** but don't do it for them. Direct the girls in setting up their tents, but allow them the accomplishment of doing it on their own. Camp is a great time for young women to learn to recognize their strengths and abilities. Along with tent set-up, ask for help setting up the rest of camp. All hands should be expected to be on deck. Set the tone early that you expect everyone to help pull their own weight while at camp. If everybody pitches in, the load will be lighter and the play time will come quicker.

Tips to Help Camp Run More Smoothly:

- **Stick to your schedule when possible,** but be prepared for some slack. Things will inevitably happen to throw you off schedule, but don't sweat it. If a massive downpour floods out your hike, fill the time with another activity or provide some down time for visiting, reading, or playing games. If dinner goes longer than planned and cuts into your evening activity, roll with it. If you miss out on an activity, but feel it has enough value to not be scratched entirely, present it to the Young Women president as a possibility for a weekday activity. Running around trying to keep everything right on schedule will only stress you out. And if the girls or leaders feel stressed, everyone will feel it.

- **Have fun!** Laugh. Sing. Play. Camp is meant to be enjoyed, not just by the girls, but by you too. It's okay to let loose and have a good time. In fact, if creating a relationship with the girls is important (and it is!) there isn't a better way to invite them to trust you than to get on their level and build a friendship. A leader may end up being the saving grace for a troubled young woman. If you don't take the time to build a relationship of respect and trust and friendship, the chances of being that critical influence a girl may need is greatly reduced.

Chapter 15

Dealing with Unhappy, Unruly, or Disrespectful Campers

*E*ven with the best planning, the most incredible activities, and the most obedient of girls, sometimes things get off course. Inevitably you've heard a story or two about an unhappy, unruly, or disrespectful camper. Don't start to panic, and don't create a doomsday attitude just yet. Yes, these things happen; after all, don't we all reserve the right to be crabby every now and then? My experience, however, has been that these little stories are the exception, not the rule. My purpose for bringing this up is to simply help you be prepared.

It's no secret that most girls today aren't exactly avid outdoors-women. In fact, other than Girls Camp, it is likely that some of them rarely spend quality time outdoors. Imagine for a moment that this is you (okay, maybe you don't have to imagine too deeply) and that all the comforts you're used to are suddenly gone. For a week! Because they don't camp, they may have had to borrow some friend or family member's sleeping bag. Because they're not used to being outside so much, the sunlight may start taking a toll on them. Or, perhaps it's the unexpected rain. Or the food. Or how about this one: maybe they're not comfortable in the company of others 24-7. The possibilities are endless, but one thing is for sure: whether they show it or not, some of your girls may have a hard time. Some of them may need some encouragement. And some of them may just have a breakdown.

So how do you handle it when the claws come out or the tears start falling? How do you help maintain peace at your camp while a tired or ornery or simply rebellious young woman seems intent to shake things up?

The answer is simple: Love her.

Love her regardless of her actions. Be positive and supportive. Encourage her to participate in something fun. Suggest ways that she might be able to help improve her situation. Help her feel important by inviting her to be your special camp helper. Or, if what she needs is some quiet alone-time, provide a safe place for her to have it. Typically, a little bit of love and patience will remedy most situations, but sometimes more is required.

Avoid gossiping about anyone at camp. If you need to talk to another leader, do so in private. Don't ever say something that might belittle a camper in front of her peers. Discourage other girls from gossiping as well. If they start to do so, gently put a stop to it. Remember that we are all precious in the sight of our Father.

Maintain a camp where the Spirit can be present at ALL TIMES. This means starting any discussion or discipline with prayer. If you can leave the situation for a minute to have a private prayer, do so. If the girl's bishop or a member of her bishopric is at camp, consult him and allow him to take the lead.

If you find yourself in a situation where you need to "improve" or discipline one of your young ladies, turn it over to the Young Women president . . . and do so in private. If it's appropriate for you to be a part of the discussion, assure that the rest of your camp is left in capable hands (like your Assistant Camp Leader's). Gently take the troubled girl away from the group, but remember to stay within open view so as to protect both of you from rumors or accusations. Involve a priesthood leader or other camp leader if you can do so without making the girl feel like she's on the defensive.

Never yell, belittle, or lose your temper. Starting with a prayer can help calm both her nerves and yours, thus setting a more appropriate mood for a non-abrasive conversation. Invite her to offer the prayer if she'd like but don't force her to do so. If she doesn't feel comfortable, offer it yourself. It might be tempting—especially if she's vocally unhappy and unpleasant—to hold a conversation without first praying; however, only after you've sincerely prayed will you be ready to deal fairly with whatever the situation may be.

Give her ample time and an appropriate environment (away from other campers) to express her feelings. Listen without interrupting, even if you don't agree with the accusations or turmoil that she presents. Stay calm and respectful, and expect the same from her. If you don't feel like you can maintain your composure, excuse yourself and ask another leader for her help.

Though it's your goal to help every girl learn and grow through camp, there may be times where it is appropriate to have a camper leave early. This is true if she has purposefully done something that is against Church standards (for example: snuck a boy into or herself out of camp), intentionally put herself or others in danger (for example: setting a tent or other structure on fire), or caused an intentional and undisputable withdrawal of the Spirit (overt meanness, excessive teasing, stealing, and so on). These are certainly extreme situations, the likes of which I have never had to experience; however, keep in mind the safety of your camp as well as the tender spirit of the young girl in question when making the decision to call her parents and send her home.

There are other times when a girl might choose to go home on her own. Again, it is your job to encourage her to stay and to help her have a positive experience, but if she is dead set on going home, allow her to call her parents. Often a call home will help put her at ease or even help her see the big picture in a way that you cannot. Other times, the call home may just solidify her decision to leave. If this is the case, allow her to arrange a ride home with her parents. Tell her you will miss her and express your love for her before she leaves, but don't guilt her into staying. A negative attitude can detract from the Spirit of the whole camp.

Chapter 16

After Camp

*J*ust because you've broken camp and loaded all the girls and gear up to head home doesn't mean your work is done. There are a few final details left.

Decide where you're going to unload all the girls' gear. If you are camping on a stake level, this may be a decision you leave to each individual ward Camp Director. Depending on the size of your group, you may choose to drop each girl off directly at her home with all of her stuff. If you have a larger group, you might want to consider having a drop time and location in the church parking lot. In this situation, parents would need to know when and where to pick up their daughter(s). This is the method that I like best. We unload all of the gear into the church parking lot where it is easily seen, and we encourage each girl to double-check to make sure she hasn't forgotten anything. By doing this, I avoid being stuck with a garage full of lost-and-found items for weeks on end. Inevitably someone will forget something, but the overall success of this method has me convinced it's the only way to go.

After all the girls are home and their gear is gone, clean and return any ward items or borrowed supplies. Doing this as soon as you get home helps you avoid losing your steam, because the second you take a shower, your motivation will evaporate. If you have leftover food, contact your stake president, bishop, or Relief Society president to see if there is someone in the stake or ward who would benefit from it. Make sure to store it safely until it can be distributed. When everything is sufficiently put away, take a shower and a long nap. Believe me, you're going to need it!

You Can't Say "Thank you" Enough

After you've caught up on your sleep, there are just a few last loose ends to tie up. In the next week or so, give thank-you notes or gifts to all of those who helped make your camp a success. Provide cards for the young women to sign for each of your priesthood leaders, camp specialists, and guest speakers. Present a special thank-you directly from yourself to each of your YCLs. Let them know how much you appreciate them. It takes a lot of help to pull off a camp; let everyone know how valuable their contribution was.

If you didn't do an award ceremony at camp, schedule one as the first weekly activity after camp. Make the activity an extension of camp. Provide a camp-related refreshment and finish up any crafts or activities you didn't have time to complete at camp.

And, finally . . . rest! For about a week, then (unless your bishop releases you), throw a smile on your face, take a deep breath, and start it all over again!

Appendices

Appendix A
Individual Packing List

- Sleeping bag
- Pillow
- Extra blanket
- Camp pad (optional)
- Soap and towel
- Wash cloth (baby wipes work good too)
- Nail file
- Toothbrush & toothpaste
- Hair brush/comb, hair bands, clips, and so on
- Mirror
- Feminine products
- Sunscreen
- Bug repellant
- Flashlight
- Secret Sister gifts
- A treat to share
- Scriptures, journal, and pen
- Camp manual
- Rain poncho
- Canteen/water bottle
- Camera
- Pocket knife (sharpening stone for 2nd year campers)
- Triangular bandage/bandana
- Jacket/sweatshirt/hoodie
- Modest shirts
- Long pants
- Pajamas
- Underclothing and socks
- 2 pairs of closed toe shoes (one to hike in)
- Sunglasses, hat/visor
- Tissue
- Small sewing kit
- Compass (optional)
- Camp chair (optional)
- Musical instrument (optional)

Depending on your camp, the following may be needed:
- Individual items needed for crafts
- Shorts or capris,
- Modest swimwear
- Coat, thermals
- Backpack
- Mess kit
- rope

Do not bring:
- iPod, cell phone, other electronics
- Bare midriff shirts/tank tops
- Perfumes or scents that might attract animals
- Bad attitudes

Appendix B

General Gear List

General Camp Gear		Kitchen Supplies
Tents		Camp stoves
Awnings (for rain/shade)		Propane bottles
Tables (for food prep, eating, crafts)		Griddle(s)
Tablecloths		Skillet(s)
Chairs (each girl should bring her own)		Water kettle(s)
Hand soap		Pans, stock pot
Hand towels		Dutch oven(s)
Anti-bacterial hand gel		Dutch oven liners/foil
Lanterns (including propane or batteries)		Dutch oven lifters
Lantern stakes/stands		Dutch oven tables
Flashlights (with extra batteries)		Charcoal
Ax and/or hatchet		Charcoal chimney(s)
Firewood		Charcoal tongs
Lighter and matches		Cooking utensils: spoons, spatulas, whisks
Roasting sticks		Cutting boards
Campfire grill		Knives (variety of sizes)
Shovel		Can opener(s)
Broom		Dishpans
All purpose cleaner(s)/wipes		Dish soap
First-aid kit		Dish cloths and towels

	Sunscreen		Mixing bowls
	Bug spray		Food storage bags and containers
	Toilet paper and facial tissue		Coolers
	Feminine products (lots of extras!)		Water jugs (one for water, one for punch)
	Craft supplies (glue guns, scissors, tape, and so on)		Plates, cups, utensils (disposable or not?)
	Activity supplies		Paper goods: napkins, paper towels
	Camp decorations		Games for downtime
	Personal gear (see Appendix A)		

Appendix C
Camp Cooking Tips and Recipes

Dutch Oven Tips:

- If your Dutch oven is new or rusty, clean and season it before camp. Seasoning is easy; it just takes time, so don't procrastinate it until the night before camp.
  - Start by cleaning it well (new Dutch ovens have a thin wax on them to prevent rust). This will be the only time you clean your Dutch oven with soap.
  - After it has thoroughly dried, coat the entire surface (inside and out) lightly with oil. Place in a 350-degree oven for one hour.
  - Remove from oven and coat entire surface for a second time with oil. Place back in oven for another hour.
  - When time is up, turn the heat off and allow the Dutch oven to cool inside the oven.
  - When Dutch oven is fully cooled, remove and lightly rub with another thin coat of oil. A properly seasoned Dutch oven should be slightly shiny but not slippery.
- Lightly oil the inside of your Dutch oven every time you store it. Place a dry paper towel inside it before putting the lid on. Store your Dutch oven in a dry location to prevent rust. If it rusts, clean and re-season it.

- A Dutch oven's patina is what creates that amazing flavor that is associated with Dutch oven cooking. Over time a dark shellac will appear; this is the patina, and it is a good thing. It may be tempting to wash the Dutch oven with soap, but doing so will prevent the patina from building. The best Dutch ovens haven't seen soap for years!

- To clean a Dutch oven, simply scrape any excess food out of it with a metal scraper or spatula then fill it with water and bring it to a simmer. Use a metal pot scrubber or plastic scraper to remove any remaining food particles. Discard dirty water. For tough, sticky messes, generously sprinkle salt in the pan then rub with a paper towel to absorb the sticky mess. Rinse with clean water then allow it to dry. When fully dry (at least 15 minutes), lightly oil.

- When cooking for camp, decide how much time you want to invest in meal clean-up. To make clean-up faster and easier, line your Dutch ovens with heavy-duty aluminum foil or with Dutch oven liners (either aluminum or parchment). Parchment linings are great for desserts and breads as they allow you to easily lift the finished product out of the pan. They also prevent the Dutch oven flavor from corrupting your sweets. For lasagnas and other non-stir-able meals, use an aluminum lining. Avoid linings for anything that might need to be stirred.

Charcoal Tips:

- If you've ever struggled to start charcoal, here's a tip that doesn't require starter fluid or a fire pit. Place your cold charcoals in a charcoal chimney then place it on top of your camp stove. Turn the flame on high for three or four minutes then turn the fuel line off. Your coals should be lit at this point, and you can remove the chimney from your stove. Make sure if you set it on ground that it is (1) out of the way so nobody is going to trip on it and burn themselves, and (2) away from anything that is combustible.

- Determining the number of coals you need can get tricky. A good rule of thumb is to take the Dutch oven size (8, 10, 12, or

14 inches) and double it. This is the number of coals you need to establish a 350 degree cooking temperature. Add or subtract one coal for every 25 degree variance. Thus, for a 12-inch Dutch oven with a cooking temperature of 350 degrees, you would need 24 coals.

- Your coals are ready when they are about 50 percent white or when you hold your hand a couple of inches above them and the heat becomes unbearable in four to five seconds.

- To determine how many coals to put on the bottom of your pan, take the pan size and subtract three. For example, a 12-inch Dutch oven would need nine coals on the bottom. Arrange the bottom coals into a ring slightly smaller than the diameter of the oven. Arrange the remaining coals evenly across the lid.

- A typical coal will last about 40 minutes after it is hot. If you are preparing something that takes longer than 40 minutes or so, consider prepping a second round of coals about 30 minutes into your cooking.

Griddle Tips:

- When using a griddle on a camp stove, be aware that you will probably have hot spots directly over the burner. Experiment with your flame size to determine the best cooking temperature. Move items around the griddle frequently for more even cooking.

- Season a cast iron griddle the same way you would a Dutch oven. The more patina you build up, the more non-stick qualities your griddle will have.

Recipes

Mountain Man Dutch Oven Breakfast

Ingredients:

- 1 (20-oz) bag hashbrowns
- 2 dozen eggs
- ¼ cup water
- 2 lbs. ground sausage
- 1 medium onion, chopped
- 8 oz. shredded cheddar cheese

Prep: Start 28 coals. (For 14" Dutch oven)

Brown hashbrowns on well-greased griddle (butter works best for this).

Mix eggs with water in a mixing bowl.

Cook sausage and onion in Dutch oven on top of camp stove until cooked through. Add hashbrowns on top of sausage/onion mix in Dutch oven. Mix together.

Pour egg mix on top. Do not stir.

Arrange 11 coals in ring on bottom of pan. Cover with lid and put remaining coals on top.

Cook until eggs are done (about 15 or 20 minutes.)

Top with cheese just before serving.

Cinnamon Dutch-Oven Pull-Aparts

Ingredients:

- Packaged frozen cinnamon roll or sweet roll dough (12-count rolls, with frosting)

The night before: Line Dutch oven with a parchment liner or foil. Spray with non-stick cooking spray. Place one package (12 rolls) frozen cinnamon roll dough in pan. Place lid on and allow to rise in a cool place overnight.

Morning: Start 28 coals (for 14" Dutch oven) or 24 coals (for 12" Dutch oven). Bake rolls for 15–20 minutes, checking frequently to avoid burning the tops. If the tops start to darken, remove coals from the top of the Dutch oven. When rolls are done, remove from pan by lifting the corners of the parchment liner or foil and place on a cutting board. Allow to cool for a few minutes, then apply frosting.

Omelets in a Bag

Ingredients:

- Eggs (enough for 2 or 3 per person)
- Onions, chopped
- Green peppers, chopped
- Ham, chopped
- Cheese, shredded
- Quart-sized plastic storage bags (one per person)
- Salt and pepper to taste

Prep: Have girls assemble the ingredients of their omelet directly in their individual bags. Add a tablespoon of water to make the eggs more fluffy. Close bag.

Mix all ingredients in the bags.

To cook, label the bags with a waterproof marker, then drop the bags in a pot of boiling water. Boil until eggs are cooked to omelet consistency. Pull bags out of water using tongs.

Chicken Fajitas (*Quick)

Ingredients:

- Chicken, sliced, pre-seasoned and pre-cooked at home then frozen.
- Onions, julienned
- Green peppers, julienned
- Flour tortillas
- Condiments: Salsa, guacamole, sour cream
- Shredded lettuce
- Shredded Mexican cheese

Place a Dutch oven (or large skillet) on top of your cooking stove. Cover bottom of pan with 1" of water. Add pre-cooked chicken, onions, and green peppers. Cover and allow chicken to warm and vegetables to soften with the steam. Stir frequently.

Serve on flour tortillas with desired toppings.

14" Dutch Oven Lasagna

Ingredients:

- 3 lbs. ground beef or ground turkey
- 1½ lbs. shredded mozzarella
- 4 eggs
- 2 (24-oz.) containers cottage cheese
- ½ c. grated Parmesan
- 2 Tbsp. garlic powder
- ¼ cup water
- 16 ounces dry lasagna noodles
- 1½ to 2 cans or bottles of spaghetti sauce
- ½ lb. shredded Italian cheeses

Prep: Start 60 coals.

Line Dutch oven with foil liner. Spray sides & bottom of liner with non-stick spray. Brown ground beef or turkey.

In mixing bowl, combine the shredded mozzarella, eggs, cottage cheese, Parmesan, and garlic powder.

Put a thin layer of spaghetti sauce and water on bottom of pan.

Layer: (*REPEAT FOR 3 LAYERS) Dry Lasagna noodles (break to make fit), spaghetti sauce, browned meat, and cheese mixture (*_The key to using dry noodles is to make sure the sauce touches BOTH sides!_). Finish top layer with a layer of noodles. Cover with spaghetti sauce. Top with shredded Italian cheeses.

Bake with 11 coals on bottom, 20 on top for 1 hour 15 minutes. (Put new coals on after 30–40 minutes.)

**For a Meatless Lasagna, follow the same instructions as above but without the meat.

Pizza Pockets (*Easy)

Ingredients:

- Bottled pizza sauce
- Shredded Italian cheese blend
- Pre-packaged pita pockets
- *Toppings:* pepperoni, ham, olives, pineapple, chopped onions, chopped peppers

Prep: Start a campfire in advance and allow it to burn into white-hot cooking coals. Set out the ingredients and allow the campers to stuff their own pizza pocket. Wrap with heavy-duty aluminum foil, label with a marker, and set on the hot coals.

Cook time: 10–15 minutes, depending on the heat of the coals and how thick the pita bread is stuffed. Assign an adult or a YCL the job of flipping the foil packets over every few minutes to help them cook evenly.

Foil Dinners

Ingredients:

- Canned cream of chicken soup
- Chicken breasts or tenderloins, or ground beef patties
- Potatoes, chopped to ½" cubes (or southern style frozen potatoes)
- Carrots, chopped to ½" cubes (or frozen carrots)
- Frozen peas
- Onions, julienned
- Seasonings such as garlic powder, garlic pepper, season salt, or lemon-pepper blends

Prep: Start a campfire in advance and allow it to burn into white-hot cooking coals. Set out the ingredients and allow the campers to create their own dinner. Tear 12" by 12" squares of heavy-duty aluminum and spray one side with non-stick cooking spray. Dollop about a tablespoon of condensed chicken soup onto foil, top with meat (chicken or beef), then apply seasonings. Add potatoes and vegetables. Finish with another dollop of soup. Wrap foil, label with a marker, and set on the hot coals.

Cook 20–30 minutes depending on the heat of the coals and the thickness of the meat. Assign an adult or a YCL the job of flipping the foil packets over every few minutes to help them cook evenly. Make sure to cook meat thoroughly to avoid food poisoning.

Dutch-Oven Apricot Chicken

(serves 6–8; multiply for the size of your camp)

Ingredients:

- 18 Chicken tenders or 6 thin-cut chicken breasts*
- 10 oz. Russian salad dressing
- 16 oz. apricot jam or preserves
- 1 (1-oz.) pkg. dry onion soup mix
- 2 carrots, sliced
- 1 (20-oz.) pineapple chunks, drained
- Uncooked instant white rice (1 cup, uncooked, per serving, so about 8 cups uncooked rice)

*Allow frozen chicken to thaw in cooler overnight.

Prep: Start 24 coals (for 12" Dutch oven) and lightly grease your Dutch oven.. In a separate pot or another Dutch oven, boil 8 cups of water for your rice. (Remember, at higher elevations it may take a while for water to boil.)

Mix Russian dressing, apricot jam, carrots, pineapple, and onion soup mix in greased Dutch oven. Add chicken.

Cook with hot coals for 45 minutes or until chicken is thoroughly cooked. (If your chicken is still frozen or thick-cut, you may need to start more coals about 15 minutes into your cooking cycle and rotate them about 30 minutes into your cooking)

In a separate Dutch oven or aluminum pan, add boiling water to dry rice as per the package instructions. Cover with lid or foil and allow to sit while the chicken cooks.

Serve chicken over rice. Spoon apricot sauce on top like gravy.

Taco Salads

Ingredients:
- Ground beef or ground turkey—about 1 lb. per 5 people
- Beans (black, pinto, or refried)—1 (16-oz.) can per 4 people
- Taco seasoning
- Lettuce
- Shredded Mexican cheese
- Olives
- Sour cream
- Salsa
- Guacamole
- Tortilla chips (individual bags work great! Smash the chips then open up the bags and build your salad inside. No plate needed!)
- Ranch dressing

Prep: Brown and season the meat. Warm the beans. (This can be done by mixing them with the cooked meat or in a separate pan if necessary.) Allow campers to build their own salads.

Dutch-Oven Enchilada Pie

Ingredients: (for a 12" Dutch oven. Serves 10–12)

- 2 lbs. ground beef or turkey
- 2 medium onions, chopped
- 2 (1-oz. or 1.5-oz.) pkgs. taco seasoning
- 2 (15-oz.) cans corn, drained
- 3 (10-oz.) cans red enchilada sauce, divided
- ¼ cup water
- 15 corn tortillas or 10 flour tortillas
- 1 lb. shredded Mexican cheese
- Toppings: Shredded lettuce, salsa, sour cream

Start 24 coals.

Brown ground meat and chopped onions in skillet. Add taco seasoning per package instructions. (This can be done before camp and frozen until the night before you need it.) Add corn and 2 cans enchilada sauce. Mix together.

Line Dutch oven with foil liner or heavy-duty foil. Spray with non-stick cooking spray.

Layer in Dutch oven:

- Start by spooning half of a can of enchilada sauce on the bottom of the pan. Top with ¼ cup water.
- Place two layers of tortillas on the bottom of the pan. Spread them to look like a lasagna. Overlapping is okay. (The very bottom layer serves as a "sacrificial" layer since it tends to burn easily, thus the extra layer.) Spoon one-third of your meat mixture on top of tortilla layer. Cover with cheese. Place a second layer of tortillas down (this time just a single layer). Cover with one-third meat mixture and cheese again. Repeat a total of three times. Finish with a top layer of tortillas and the remaining half can of enchilada sauce. Generously cover with cheese.

Bake with 9 coals on bottom and 15 coals on top. Bake for 30 minutes or until cheese is melted all the way through.

Dutch-Oven Chicken-n-Biscuits

(12" Dutch oven, serves 8–10)
Ingredients:

- 8–10 thin-cut chicken breasts
- 2 (6-oz.) pkgs. chicken stuffing mix
- 2 (10.5-oz.) cans cream of chicken soup
- 16 oz. sour cream
- 10 oz. frozen vegetable mix (corn, peas, carrots)
- 2 (10-count) cans refrigerated biscuit dough

Start 24 coals. Line Dutch oven with aluminum lining or a double layer of heavy-duty aluminum foil. Spray with non-stick cooking spray.

Mix stuffing mix, chicken soup, sour cream, and vegetables in Dutch oven. Place chicken breasts in a single layer on top. Bake for 30 minutes or until chicken is almost done.

Add biscuit dough to top of chicken. Bake for another 15 minutes or until biscuits are done.

Scones

Ingredients:

- Frozen roll dough (thawed)
- Canola or vegetable oil (for frying)
- Toppings: Jams, butter, honey butter, cinnamon-sugar

Fill Dutch oven or deep, heavy-bottomed pan ¾ full of oil and heat to 400 degrees (a low boil).

Smash dough balls into flat pucks and drop in hot oil. Cook both sides until lightly browned. Remove from oil and place on a paper-towel lined plate to allow excess grease to drain off of them. Cool slightly and top with favorite topping.

Navajo Tacos

Ingredients:

- Frozen roll dough (thawed)
- Canola or vegetable oil (for frying)
- Canned chili
- Toppings: Sour cream, diced tomatoes, shredded lettuce, diced onions, sliced olives, shredded cheese

Follow instructions above for Scones, except double the size of your scones by kneading two dough balls together before frying them.

Warm chili in a pan. Top warm scones with chili, tomatoes, lettuce, onions, cheese, and sour cream.

Banana Boats

Ingredients:

- Bananas
- Chocolate bars or chocolate chips
- Peanut butter or peanut butter cup candy
- Marshmallows

Prepare a fire and allow it to burn until coals are white-hot and flames are low.

Lay a banana on its side and slice it lengthwise through the top layer of peel and the flesh of the banana. Do not slice through the bottom layer of peel. Insert desired fillings: chocolate, peanut butter, marshmallows (or any combination) into the slit. Close up banana and wrap it with two layers of aluminum foil. Place in hot coals for about 10 minutes to allow the candy to melt.

Using tongs, remove from coals. Place on a plate, open up the foil, and eat directly out of the peel with a spoon.

Dump Cakes

Ingredients: (For a 12" Dutch oven. Double for a 14" Dutch oven)

- 1 boxed cake mix, any flavor
- 2 (25–30-oz.) cans fruit, drained, or 2 cans pie filling
- 1 can of lemon-lime soda
- 1 cube (½ cup) butter
- ¼ cup brown sugar or cinnamon sugar
- Ice cream or whipped topping, for serving

Start 24 coals. Line Dutch oven with parchment liner or aluminum foil. (Be careful to tightly seal any seams in the foil or you will lose your juices and create a sticky mess in your pan!) Spray with non-stick cooking spray.

Dump drained fruit/pie filling in bottom of pan. Cover with dry cake mix. Pour can of soda on top, paying special attention to the edges. Dot with butter. Sprinkle brown sugar or cinnamon sugar on top.

Bake for 30 min.

Serve warm. Top with ice cream or whipped topping.

Fruit and cake combination suggestions:

- Chocolate cake and cherry pie filling
- Yellow cake, blueberry pie filling, and crushed pineapple
- Yellow cake and peaches
- Yellow cake, pears, and blueberry pie filling
- White cake and cherry and blueberry pie fillings
- White cake, crushed pineapple, and cherry pie filling
- Spice cake and apple pie filling

Pineapple Upside-Down Cake

Ingredients:

- ½ cup butter
- 1½ cup brown sugar
- 1 (20-oz.) can pineapple slices, drain juice and set aside for cake mix prep
- 10 maraschino cherries
- 1 pineapple cake mix, prepared as directed on package, using pineapple juice in place of liquids.

Start 24 coals. Line Dutch oven with 2 layers of heavy-duty aluminum foil.

Melt butter in bottom of foil-lined pan. Remove from heat and sprinkle brown sugar to cover the melted butter. Arrange pineapple rings around bottom of pan. Place a cherry in each pineapple center.

Pour prepared cake batter on top and bake as directed on mix (you may have to add 5 minutes.)

Cool for 10 minutes then remove from pan by lifting out the foil lining. Turn over onto a large plate or cutting board.

Appendix D:

Camp Song Lyrics

Contents

Action Songs:

Silly Songs:

Rounds:

Quiet Songs:

Action Songs

Bananas

Bananas unite! *(Everyone stand up. Place hands together straight up over head)*

Peel bananas, peel, peel bananas *(Open arms and lower them to your sides)* *(Repeat)*

Smash bananas, smash, smash bananas *(Clap hands)* *(Repeat)*

Eat bananas, eat, eat bananas *(Stuff imaginary banana in mouth and sing with mouth full)* *(Repeat)*

Go bananas, GO GO bananas *(Do a crazy dance)* *(Repeat)*

And you peel to the left *(Place hands together over head then "peel" left arm)*

And you peel to the right *("peel" right arm)*

And you peel your banana *(Place hands together over head then "peel" both arms)*

And you "uh" (or yum) take a bite!! *(Take imaginary bite)* Chomp!

Boogaloo
(Several people can line up beside the song leader with their arms around each others' shoulders. Campers should do the same facing the leaders)

Leader: Drop the beat!
Campers: Chh chh chh . . . (stomp feet to beat)

Leader: Let me see you boogaloo!
Campers: WHAT'S THAT YOU SAY?

Leader: I said let me see you boogaloo!!
Campers: WHAT'S THAT YOU SAY?

Leader: I said let me see you boogaloo!!!
Campers: What's that you say?

All: ooh ahh ahh, ahh, ooh, ahh, ahh ahh, ooh (while dancing around)

Leader: Boogaloo! (everyone moves back in line stomping and chanting chh chh . . .)

Other verses: Funky Chicken, Superman, Frankenstein, Surfer Dude, Ballerina, Egyptian, Fry like bacon

C-h-i-c-k-e-n
(Often sung at the end of Rufus Rastus)

(Shape each letter with your arms as you sing it)

C—that's the way it begins.

H—that's the next letter in.

I—I am the third.

C—that's the season of the bird.

K—that old letter's my friend.

E—now we're nearin' the end.

C–H–I–C–K–E–N

That is the way you spell CHICKEN.

Down by the Banks

(Sit in a circle with your right hand face-up on top of your neighbor's left hand. In a clock-wise fashion, one participant at a time slaps her neighbor's hand. Whomever's hand is slapped at the end of each round with the word "Kerplop" is out. Repeat until you have a single singer left in the circle.)

Down by the banks of the hanky panky

Where the bull frogs jump from bank to banky

With a hip, hop, hippity hop,

Leap off a lily pad and go Kerplop!

Down by the banks of the hanky panky

Where the bull frogs jump from bank to banky

With a flip, flop, flippity flop,

Leap off a lily pad and go Kerplop!

Down by the banks of the hanky panky

Where the bull frogs jump from bank to banky

With an Eep! Ipe! Oop! Op!

Ee-sock-a-dilly and a Kerplop!

Father Abraham
(Repeat several times, each time naming a
different body part to add to the mix.)

Father Abraham had seven sons
Seven sons had Father Abraham
And they never laughed,
And they never cried,
All they did was go like this . . .
With a right *(shake right arm)*

*(Repeat from beginning then add each of the following verses one at a time
until you are doing all eight actions)*—
And a left *(shake left arm)*
And a right *(shake right leg)*
And a left *(shake left leg)*
And a bump *(bump back ends with your neighbor)*
And a shake *(shake head)*
And a turn *(turn around)*

*(On the last time through, complete each action then collapse to the ground
with exhaustion)*

Head, Shoulders, Knees, and Toes
Chords for guitar or other accompaniment are included above each lines.

(Touch each body part as you sing its name. Repeat several times increasing your speed each time.)

G
Head, shoulders, knees and toes, knees and toes, knees and toes.
G D
Head, shoulders, knees and toes,
G C
Eyes, ears, mouth and nose.

Head, Shoulders, Knees, and Toes
(Japanese version)

Atama, kata hiza, ashi
Hiza ashi, hiza ashi
Atama, kata hiza ashi,
Me mimi kuchi hana

If All the Raindrops

C G7 C
If all the raindrops were lemon drops and gumdrops *(make raindrops with fingers)*
G7 C
Oh, what a rain it would be!
C F C G7
I'd stand outside with my mouth open wide . . . *(open mouth to sky)*
C F C G7
Ah, ah, ah, ah, ah, ah, ah, ah, ah, ah!
C G7 C
If all the raindrops were lemon drops and gumdrops *(make raindrops with fingers)*
G7 C
Oh, what a rain it would be!

If all the snowflakes were Hershey bars and milkshakes *(make snowflakes with fingers)*
Oh what a storm it would be!
I'd stand outside with my mouth open wide . . . *(open mouth to sky)*
Ah, ah, ah, ah, ah, ah, ah, ah, ah ,ah!

If all the snowflakes were Hershey bars and milkshakes *(make snowflakes with fingers)*
Oh what a storm it would be!

If all the dirt clods were hamburgers and hotdogs *(make dirt clods with hands)*
Oh what a world this would be!
I'd stand outside with my mouth open wide . . . *(open mouth to sky)*
Ah, ah, ah, ah, ah, ah, ah, ah, ah ,ah!
If all the dirt clods were hamburgers and hotdogs *(make dirt clods with hands)*
Oh what a world this would be!

Jaws/Shark

C
Fetal shark - doot doot, doot doot. (make tiny jaws with your thumb and forefinger)
Fetal shark - doot doot, doot doot.
G7
Fetal shark - doot doot, doot doot.
C
Fetal shark - doot doot, doot doot.

Baby shark . . . . (make small jaws with your hands)

Child shark . . . . (make slightly bigger jaws with your hands)

Mama shark . . . . (open your "jaws" up to your elbows)

Papa shark . . . . (open your "jaws" all the way to your shoulders)

A lady swimmer . . . . (pretend swim)

C'mon in . . . the water's fine . . . . (wave a welcome)

Shark swimming . . . . (hand on head like a fin, imitate shark swim)

Shark attack - aaaaahhhhh (giant snap with shark jaws)

Happy shark . . . (hand on head like a fin, imitate shark swim)

Little Bunny Foo Foo
(Act out each action as you sing it)

C G7 C
All: Little Bunny Foo Foo hoppin' through the forest,
C G7 C
scoopin' up the field mice and boppin' them on the head
(Spoken) Down came the good Fairy and she said:
(Sung) "Little Bunny Foo Foo I don't want to see you scoopin' up the
field mice and boppin them on the head."

Leader: "Little Bunny Foo Foo," she said, "I'm going to give you three
chances and if you continue to scoop up the field mice and bop the on
the head, I'm going to turn you into a goon! Next day . . .

All: Little Bunny Foo Foo hopping through the forest,
scoopin' up the field mice and boppin' them on the head
Down came the good Fairy and she said:
"Little Bunny Foo Foo I don't want to see you scoopin' up the field mice
and boppin them on the head."

Leader: "Little Bunny Foo Foo," she said, "I gave you three chances and
now you only have two left. If you continue to scoop up the field mice
and bop them on the head, I'm going to turn you into a goon!" Next
day . . .

All: Little Bunny Foo Foo hopping through the forest,
scoopin' up the field mice and boppin' them on the head
Down came the good Fairy and she said:
"Little Bunny Foo Foo I don't want to see you scoopin' up the field mice
and boppin them on the head."

Leader: "Little Bunny Foo Foo," she said, "I gave you three chances and
now you only have one left. If you continue to scoop up the field mice
and bop them on the head, I'm going to turn you into a goon!" Next
day . . .

All: Little Bunny Foo Foo hopping through the forest,

scoopin' up the field mice and boppin' them on the head
Down came the good Fairy and she said:
"Little Bunny Foo Foo I don't want to see you scoopin' up the field mice and boppin them on the head."

Leader: "Little Bunny Foo Foo," she said, "I gave you three chances and now you've use them all up. So now I'm going to have to turn you into a goon!" Moral of the story: Hare today, goon tomorrow.

My Aunt Came Back

(Leader sings each line then group echoes. Actions are cumulative, so as each new verse is sung new actions are added to the others.)

My aunt came back *(repeat)*
From old Japan *(repeat)*
And brought with her *(repeat)*
An old hand fan *(repeat)*

My aunt came back *(repeat)*
From old Algiers *(repeat)*
And brought with her *(repeat)*
Some old hand shears *(repeat)*

My aunt came back *(repeat)*
From Holland too *(repeat)*
And brought with her *(repeat)*
Some wooden shoes *(repeat)*

My aunt came back *(repeat)*
From the New York Fair *(repeat)*
And brought with her *(repeat)*
A rocking chair *(repeat)*

My aunt came back *(repeat)*
From Kalamazoo *(repeat)*
And brought for me *(repeat)*
Some gum to chew *(repeat)*

My aunt came back *(repeat)*
From the monkey zoo *(repeat)*
And brought for me *(repeat)*
Some nuts like you!

Noah's Song

C F
The Lord said to Noah there's gonna be a floody, floody.
C F
The Lord said to Noah there's gonna be a floody, floody.
C G7
Get those animals *(clap!)* out of the muddy, muddy,
C G7 C
Children of the Lord.

CHORUS:
C F
So, rise and shine and give God his glory, glory.
C F
Rise and shine and give God his glory, glory.
C C7 F
Rise and shine and give God his glory, glory.
C G7 C
Children of the Lord.

So, Noah he built him, he built him an arky, arky.
So Noah, he built him, he built him an arky, arky.
Built it out of *(clap!)* hickory barky, barky.
Children of the Lord

–CHORUS–

The animals they came on, they came on by twosies, twosies
The animals they came on, they came on by twosies, twosies
Elephants and (clap!) kangaroosies, roosies
Children of the Lord.

–CHORUS–

It rained and poured for forty daysies, daysies
It rained and poured for forty daysies, daysies
Almost drove those (clap!) animals crazy, crazy
Children of the Lord

132

–CHORUS–

The sun came out and dried up the landy, landy
The sun came out and dried up the landy, landy
Everything was *(clap!)* fine and dandy, dandy
Children of the Lord.

–CHORUS–

The animals they came out, they came out in threesies, threesies
The animals they came out, they came out in threesies, threesies,
Must have been those *(clap!)* birds and beesies, beesies
Children of the Lord.

–CHORUS–

This is the end of, the end of our story, story
This is the end of, the end of our story, story
Everything was *(clap!)* hunky-dory, dory
Children of the Lord.

–CHORUS–

Princess Pat
(Each line is sung by a leader then repeated by the entire group)

The Princess Pat *(Strike an Egyptian pose)*
Lived in a tree. *(Arms over head like branches)*
She sailed across *(Rolling wave motion with one hand)*
The seven seas *(Show 7 fingers then make the letter "C" with one hand)*
She sailed across *(Rolling wave motion with one hand)*
The channel too, *(Two hands tracing a channel, then two fingers)*
And brought with her, *(Throw a sack over your shoulder)*
A rig-a-bamboo. *(Wiggle your arms and bend your knees as you move down)*

CHORUS:
A rig-a-bamboo, *(same as before)*
Now what is that? *(Shrug shoulders, hold out hands)*
It's something made *(Bang one fist on top of the other)*
By the Princess Pat. *(Egyptian pose)*
It's red and gold *(Twirl one arm down by your hip)*
And purple too *(Flip hands out in front of you)*
That's why it's called *(Cup hands in front of mouth as if to shout)*
A rig-a-bamboo. *(same as before)*

Now Captain Jack *(Salute)*
Had a mighty fine crew. *(Salute several times)*
They sailed across *(Wave action)*
The channel too. *(Two hands tracing a channel, then two fingers)*
His ship did sink, *(Plug nose with one hand and wave other hand over head as you bend your knees and "sink" down)*
And so will you, *(Point to others in the group)*
If you don't take *(Throw an invisible bag over your shoulder)*
A rig-a-bamboo. *(Same as before)*

–CHORUS–

Silly Songs

An Austrian Went Yodeling

D A7 D A7 D
Oh, an Austrian went yodeling on a mountain so high.
A7 D
When along came a cuckoo bird interrupting his cry.

CHORUS:
A7
Oh-lay-ah
D A7
Oh lay rah hee-hee, oh lay rah cuckoo, cuckoo
D
Oh lay rah hee-hee, oh lay rah cuckoo, cuckoo
D A7
Oh lay rah hee-hee, oh lay rah cuckoo, cuckoo
D
Oh lay rah hee-hee, oh

Repeat first verse, replacing the cuckoo bird each time with: Skier, Avalanche, Billy Goat, St. Bernard, Road Runner, Grizzly Bear, Two lovers, A mother, and so on.

The Bear Song

Leader (Group echoing):
The other day *(echo)* . . . I saw a bear *(echo)*
A great big bear *(echo)* . . . A way up there *(echo)*

Everyone in unison:
The other day, I saw a bear, A great big bear, a way up there.

Continue the above pattern for the remaining verses:

I looked at him . . . He looked at me,
I sized up him . . . He sized up me.

He says to me . . . Why don't you run?
I see you ain't . . . Got any gun.

I said to him . . . That's a good idea
So come on feet . . . Let's get out of here.

And so I ran . . . Away from there.
But right behind . . . Me was the bear.

But ahead of me . . . there was a tree.
A great big tree . . . Oh, Glory be!

But the lowest branch . . .. Was ten feet up.
I'd have to trust . . . My luck to jump.

And so I jumped . . . Into the air.
But I missed that branch . . . A way up there.

Now don't you fret . . . Now don't you frown.
'Cause I caught that branch . . . on the way back down.

That's all there is . . . There ain't no more.
Unless I meet . . . That bear once more.

Boom Chicka Boom

I said a boom chicka boom *(echo)*
I said a boom chicka boom *(echo)*
I said a boom chicka rocka, chicka rocka, chicka boom *(echo)*
Oh yeah *(echo)*
Uh huh *(echo)*
One more time *(echo)*
_____ style *(echo)*

Different styles: Loud, Whisper, Southern, Valley Girl, Attitude, British, Rocket, Harley, Teacher, and so on

Valley Girl Style: I said like boom chicka boom
I said a totally boom chicka boom
I said like boom chicka like rocka chicka like gag me with a spoon

Baseball Style: I said a boom chicka boom . . .
I said a boom chicka rocka hit that softball to the moon.

Race Car Style: I said a vroom shifta vroom . . .
I said a vroom shifta grind-a shifta grind-a shifta vroom

Rocket Style: I said a moon shoot the moon . . .
I said a moon blast-me shoot-me blast-me shoot-me-to-the-moon

Janitor style: I said a broom sweep-a-broom . . .
I said a broom sweep a-mop-a sweep-a-mop-a sweep-a-broom

Parent Style: I said a boom GO TO YOUR ROOM . . .
I said a boom GO TO YOUR ROOM and don't come out 'til next June.

Surfer Style: I said a dude chicka dude . . .
I said a dude chicka wipe out chicka WHOA chicka dude

Harley Style: I said a Vroom Squeela Vroom . . .
I said a Vroom, Theres a Coppa, Betta Stoppa Chicka Vroom

The Cat Came Back
(Guitar Chords are the same for every line.)

Em D C B7
Old mister Johnson had troubles of his own,
He had a yellow cat, that wouldn't leave home
He tried and he tried to get that cat away
He gave him to a man who was going far away.

CHORUS:
But the cat came back, the very next day,
Oh the cat came back, they thought he was a goner.
But the cat came back, he just wouldn't stay away.

The man around the corner said he'd shoot that cat on sight.
So he loaded up his shotgun with nails and dynamite.
He waited and he waited for that cat to come around.
Ninety-seven pieces of that man was all they found.

–CHORUS–

He gave a little boy a ten pound note.
Take him out in a river, take him out in a boat.
He tied a rope around his neck, he must have weighed a pound
Next day they dragged the river, for the poor boy had drowned.

–CHORUS–

The H-bomb exploded the very next day.
The A-bomb exploded in the very same way.
Russia went, China went, then the USA,
The human race was ended without a chance to pray.

–CHORUS–

Clementine

D
In a cavern, in a canyon
A7
Excavating for a mine
G D
Lived a miner, Forty-niner
A7 D
And his daughter, Clementine.

CHORUS:
D
Oh my darlin', oh my darlin'
A7
Oh my darlin' Clementine.
G D
You are lost and gone forever
A7 D
Dreadful sorry, Clementine.
Light she was and like a feather
And her shoes were number nine
Wearing boxes without topses.
Sounds like my Clementine.

–CHORUS–

Drove the ducklings to the water
Every morning just at nine
Hit her foot against a splinter
Fell into the foamy brine.

–CHORUS–

Ruby lips above the water
Blowing bubbles soft and fine
But alas, I was no swimmer
Couldn't save my Clementine.

–CHORUS–

How I missed her, how I missed her
How I missed my Clementine.
Till I kissed her little sister
And forgot my Clementine.

–CHORUS–

Donut Shop
(Sung to the tune of "Do Your Ears Hang Low")

Oooooooh, I ran around the corner, and I ran around the block.
And I ran right into a baker's shop.
I picked up a donut, right out of the hot grease
And I handed the lady a five-cent piece.
She looked at the nickel, and she looked at me
And she said, "Kind sir, can't you plainly see,
There's a hole in the nickel, and it goes clear through."
Says I, "There's a hole in the donut too
Thanks for the donut, Toodle-loo!"

Eddie Kucha

CHORUS:
E C D7 G
Eddie Kucha-Kacha-Kama-Tosa-Nara-Tosa-Noka-Sama-Kama-Wacky-
Brown. Who?
E C D7 G
Eddie Kucha-Kacha-Kama-Tosa-Nara-Tosa-Noka-Sama-Kama-Wacky-
Brown. Who?
G C
Fell into the well, fell into the well,
D7 G
Fell into the deep dark well.
C D7 G C D7 C
Susie Jones, milking in the barn,
C D7 G D D7
Saw him fall and ran inside to tell her ma that . . .

–CHORUS–

Susie's ma, making cradklin' bread
Called old Joe to tell him that her Susie said that:

–CHORUS–

Then old Joe put his plow aside,
Grabbed his cane, and hobbled into to town to say that:

–CHORUS–

To the well everybody came
What a shame, it took so long to say his name, that:

–CHORUS–

Who?
Eddie Kucha-Kacha-Kama-Tosa-Nara-Tosa-Noka-
Sama-Kama-Wacky-Brown.
Drowned.

J-E-L-L-O

Oh, the big red letters stand for the Jello Family.
Oh, the big red letters stand for the Jello Family.
It's Jello, yum, yum, yum!
Jello Pudding, yum, yum!
Jello Ta-pi-oca pudding
Try all three!
Yum! Yum!

John Jacob Jingleheimer Schmidt

C
John Jacob Jingleheimer Schmidt
G7
His name is my name too.
Whenever I go out, the people always shout:
C
"There goes John Jacob Jingleheimer Schmidt!"
C
Tra la la la la la . . ..

(Repeat song at various volumes)

Pile of Tin
(This can be sung as a two part round.
Start the second group after the word "tin")

Actions: Pull on ear for the word "honk," shake head for the word "rattle," put palm of hand on chin for the word "crash."

I'm a little pile of tin
Nobody knows what shape I'm in
Got four wheels and a running board
I'm a four door – I'm a Ford.
Honk, honk - rattle, rattle, rattle, – crash – beep, beep
Honk, honk - rattle, rattle, rattle, – crash – beep, beep
Honk, honk - rattle, rattle, rattle, – crash – beep, beep
Honk, honk - rattle, rattle, rattle, – crash – beep, beep

I'm a little acorn brown
Lying on the cold, cold ground
Everybody steps on me
That is why I'm cracked you see
I'm a nut, in a rut. I'm a nut in a rut, so what.

Grandpa's beard is growing long
Growing longer day by day
Grandma chews it in her sleep
Thinks she's eating shredded wheat
I'm a nut, in a rut. I'm a nut in a rut, so what.

Rufus Rastus
(Often coupled with C-h-i-c-k-e-n)

Rufus Rastus Johnston Brown
What ya gonna do when the rent comes round?
What ya gonna say, how ya gonna pay?
You ain't been workin' since the judgment day.
Oh you know and I know the rent means dough,
The landlord's gonna kick up right out in the snow
Rufus Rastus Johnston Brown
What ya gonna do when the rent comes round?

Sippin' Cider

D
The cutest boy *(echo)*, I ever saw *(echo)*
A7 D
Was sippin' ci–*(echo)* der through a straw *(echo)*
D G
The cutest boy, I ever saw
D A7
Was sippin' cider through a straw.

I asked him if *(echo)* he'd show me how *(echo)*
To sip that ci–*(echo)* der through a straw *(echo)*
I asked him if he'd show me how
To sip that cider through a straw.

He said of course *(echo)*, he'd show me how *(echo)*
To sip that ci–*(echo)* der through a straw *(echo)*
He said of course he's show me how
To sip that cider through a straw.

First cheek to cheek *(echo)*, then jaw to jaw *(echo)*
We sipped that ci-*(echo)* der through a straw.
First cheek to cheek, then jaw to jaw
We sipped that cider through a straw.

Then all at once *(echo)*, that straw would slip *(echo)*
And we'd sip ci–*echo)* der lipe to lip *(echo)*
Then all at once that straw would slip
And we'd slip cider lip to lip.

That's how I got *(echo)*, my mother-in-law *(echo)*
And 49 kids *(echo)*, that call me ma *(echo)*.
That's how I got my mother-in-law
And 49 kids that call me ma.

(cont. on next page)

The moral of *(echo)* this story is *(echo)*
Don't sip that ci–*(echo)* der through a straw *(echo)*
The moral of this story is
Don't sip that cider, drink ROOT BEER!

Rounds

Spider's Web

(Sing the first stanza together then while half the group sings the second stanza, the other half re-sings the first one.)

There's a web like a spider's web
Made of silver light and shadow
Spun by the moon in my room at night.
It's a web, made to catch my dream
Hold it tight 'til I awaken
As if to tell me, my dream is all right.

Down in the Valley,
There is a meadow
Down by the old oak tree,
And in that meadow
There is a river,
Where my love flows free.

I Love the Mountains
(Start round at asterisks **)

I love the mountains, I love the rolling hills,
**I love the clovers, I love the daffodils,
I love the fireside, when all the lights are low.
Boom de ah da, boom de ah da,
Boom de ah da, boom de ay.

Quiet Songs

Circle of Friendship

Ours is a circle, a circle of friendship.
And just like a circle, it goes on and on.
Endless eternal, this circle of friendship.
Enter our circle, for here you belong.
Laughing and singing our good times together,
and sharing the blessings sent from above.
You and I sharing this circle of friendship,
Join as we open our circle of love.

Kumbaya

C F C
Kumbaya, my Lord, kumbaya.
 G7 C G7
Kumbaya, my Lord, kumbaya.
C F C
Kumbaya, my Lord, kumbaya.
F C G7 C
Oh, Lord, kumbaya.

    Someone's singing, my Lord, kum ba ya.
    Someone's singing, my Lord, kum ba ya.
    Someone's singing, my Lord, kum ba ya.
    Oh, Lord, kum ba ya.
    *Other verses: Someone's crying/Someone's praying.

Misty's Song

Tell me the reason I was born to roam.
Tell me the reason I am so far from home.
Tell me the reason only birds can fly.
Tell me the reason I was born just to die.

How many mountains will I have to climb?
How many memories will I leave behind?
How many daydreams will I make come true?
How many heartbreaks until I find you?

There is a valley called Peace of Mind.
There is a river running right by its side.
There is a moment of glory so new.
There is Eternity to spend loving you.

Other Quiet Songs:

A Child's Prayer (*LDS Children's Songbook* #12)

He Sent His Son (*LDS Children's Songbook* #34)

Candle on the Water (from Disney's *Pete's Dragon*)

Eidelweiss (from Rodgers & Hammerstein's *The Sound of Music*)

The Spirit of God (LDS Hymns #2)

Walk Tall (music and words by Jamie Glenn)

Sources:

Young Women Camp Manual (Salt Lake City: Intellectual Reserve, 2002)

Young Women Camp: A Guide for Priesthood and Young Women Leaders (Salt Lake City: Intellectual Reserve, 2007)

Church Handbook; section 10, Young Women: section 13, Activities: and section 21.1.20, Guest Speakers or Instructors

For the Strength of Youth (Salt Lake City: Intellectual Reserve, 2011)

Young Women Personal Progress (Salt Lake City: Intellectual Reserve, 2008)

Notes

Notes

Notes
....

Notes

About the Author

S tephanie Connelley Worlton lives in the shadow of the Rocky Mountains, where she enjoys frequent opportunities to observe nature and appreciate God's magnificent creations. She is a seasoned Camp Director, an avid Scouter, and a devoted youth leader. Aside from the busy schedule she keeps as a wife and mother of four, Stephanie enjoys organizing, interior design, gardening, carpentry, painting, and being involved with the youth of our rising generation.

all of me